YOU CAN BET ON IT

Published by Hartley Publications
P.O. Box 100, Devizes, Wiltshire, SN10 4TE

ISBN 1873313225

Acknowledgements

Ryan Bliss, Gary Davis, Oscar Yeadon, Ashley White, Dan Downie.

First published 2003

Sixth edition: 2015

P.O.Box 100
Devizes
Wiltshire
SN10 4TE

Typeset and make-up by Wentrow Media.

Contents

Introduction

The purpose of this book is to enhance your enjoyment of betting on horseracing, football and the lottery.

Betting on horses on a Saturday has long been a British institution and that tradition continues today. Whilst this book does not exclusively deal with betting on any particular day, it is fair to say that Saturday is the most popular day with punters, and opportunities are aplenty.

The majority of Saturday punters do not go to the races. The television coverage is so good that many prefer to watch at home and rarely go to the races.

Many punters have their favourite jockeys and trainers and they acquire an affinity that leads to betting on every horse ridden or trained by them. Whilst it's entertaining, it's not exactly scientific.

By increasing your activity on a Saturday, you instantly increase the entertainment value and you don't have to bet more money than you normally do.

There's an assumption that you will never bet more than you can afford to lose. The idea is that betting should always be treated as an entertainment.

Improving Your Chances

Whilst betting should be treated as an entertainment, every punter, quite rightly, wants to WIN. So how can you try to improve your chances of winning?

Firstly, you need to understand how betting works and pages 9 and 10 will explain it in simple terms.

Once you have grasped the fact that the odds offered by bookmakers are stacked in their favour, your best chance of making a profit is to look for value.

Quite often, the favourite in the race represents poor value for money, so it stands to reason that taking the favourite out of the equation could help stack the odds in your favour. The trouble is that quite often the favourite has the best chance on form, so the next step is to look for competitive races, where the favourite is more vulnerable.

Races on a Saturday are usually more competitive because the owners' prize-money is greater. The racing industry cashes in on the popularity of Saturday racing in many different ways. Punters can benefit from this more competitive racing, both in terms of betting opportunities and entertainment value.

potensis
BETFRED

Making the Book Work for You

The term 'book' is derived from the early days when people started to engage in the profession of offering bets on the outcome of horse races.

Where one horse was perceived to have a better chance of beating another, different odds were offered on the outcome.

The bets taken on each horse were written down in a ledger, with different columns on the page, for each horse in the race.

The 'liability' (the amount the bookmaker would need to pay out and the amount of profit/loss he would make) could then be quickly calculated.

These ledgers became known as 'the book' and the people taking the bets, became known as 'bookmakers'.

Bookmakers became the 'layers' of the odds (those who laid/offered) and the people who accepted the bookmakers invitation to back the horses at the advertised odds, became the 'backers' (punters).

Bookmakers had to be good mathematicians, otherwise they would risk losing money to clever punters.

The original principle of how bookmakers made the 'book' work for them, involved the creation of an 'overround'. This principle is still very much alive today and indeed it is recommended that punters understand it.

The 'overround' is the potential profit margin that a bookmaker can make on a race (or indeed any outcome of any event).

The bookmaker offers odds on each horse, for example, Evens, 3-1, 5-1, 12-1, 20-1 etc.... however, all odds are really percentages. Each set of odds has its own percentage figure and these can be found on the grid on page 11.

The bookmaker HAS to always ensure that all the percentages (all the odds) add up to a figure of 100% or greater, otherwise a punter could simply place a stake on each horse in the race, in relation to the percentage offered, to GUARANTEE a profit, NO MATTER WHICH HORSE WINS THE RACE.

Taking a four-horse race as an example; the odds offered are Evens Green Berry, 7-2 Yellow Peril, 4-1 Red Cherry, 9-2 Blue Bottle.

Using the grid, you will quickly see that in percentage terms Evens = 50%, 7-2 = 22.22%, 4-1 = 20% and 9-2 = 18.18%. The total in this example adds up to 110.40%. The difference of 10.40% above the balanced book (100%) represents the potential profit for the bookmaker, but for the punter it means that the odds are stacked against him to the tune of 10.40%. Or in other words, every horse in the race has potentially been priced at poor value.

As a punter, the trick is (and it's not easy) to try and capture perceived good value. In other words, if there was a horse priced at 3-1 (25%) and you thought it had a 50% chance of winning (Evens), then the 25% on offer could be really good value.

Quite often, the favourite in a horse race represents poor value, particularly when it's a competitive race. If you take the favourite out of the equation, then you can sometimes have the chance of getting really good value on many of the other horses in the race. The key word here is 'chance'.

The theory is that in the long-term you have a better chance of beating the bookmaker if you keep looking for 'good value'.

ODDS PERCENTAGES

Odds	% chance of winning	% chance of not winning	Odds	% chance of winning	% chance of not winning
1-20	95.24	4.76	**6-4**	40.00	60.00
1-16	94.12	5.88	**13-8**	38.10	61.90
1-15	93.75	6.25	**7-4**	36.36	63.64
1-14	93.33	6.67	**15-8**	34.78	65.22
1-13	92.86	7.14	**2-1**	33.33	66.67
1-12	92.31	7.69	**85-40**	32.00	68.00
1-11	91.67	8.33	**9-4**	30.77	69.23
1-10	90.91	9.09	**5-2**	28.57	71.43
1-9	90.00	10.00	**11-4**	26.67	73.33
2-17	89.47	10.53	**3-1**	25.00	75.00
1-8	88.89	11.11	**100-30**	23.08	76.92
2-15	88.24	11.76	**7-2**	22.22	77.78
1-7	87.50	12.50	**4-1**	20.00	80.00
2-13	86.67	13.33	**9-2**	18.18	81.82
1-6	85.71	14.29	**5-1**	16.67	83.33
2-11	84.62	15.38	**11-2**	15.38	84.62
1-5	83.33	16.67	**6-1**	14.29	85.71
2-9	81.82	18.18	**13-2**	13.33	86.67
1-4	80.00	20.00	**7-1**	12.50	87.50
2-7	77.78	22.22	**15-2**	11.76	88.24
30-100	76.92	23.08	**8-1**	11.11	88.89
1-3	75.00	25.00	**17-2**	10.53	89.47
4-11	73.33	26.67	**9-1**	10.00	90.00
2-5	71.43	28.57	**10-1**	9.09	90.91
4-9	69.23	30.77	**11-1**	8.33	91.67
40-85	68.00	32.00	**12-1**	7.69	92.31
1-2	66.67	33.33	**13-1**	7.14	92.86
8-15	65.22	34.78	**14-1**	6.67	93.33
4-7	63.64	36.36	**15-1**	6.25	93.75
8-13	61.90	38.10	**16-1**	5.88	94.12
4-6	60.00	40.00	**20-1**	4.76	95.24
8-11	57.89	42.11	**22-1**	4.35	95.65
4-5	55.56	44.44	**25-1**	3.85	96.15
5-6	54.55	45.45	**33-1**	2.94	97.06
10-11	52.38	47.62	**40-1**	2.44	97.56
Evens	50.00	50.00	**50-1**	1.96	98.04
11-10	47.62	52.38	**66-1**	1.49	98.51
6-5	45.45	54.55	**80-1**	1.23	98.77
5-4	44.44	55.56	**100-1**	0.99	99.01
11-8	42.11	57.89			

The Racecard

Presentation of the day's race cards tend to differ slightly between newspapers, but the jargon is actually very similar. This is a typical newspaper race layout, which should act as a useful guide for the beginner.

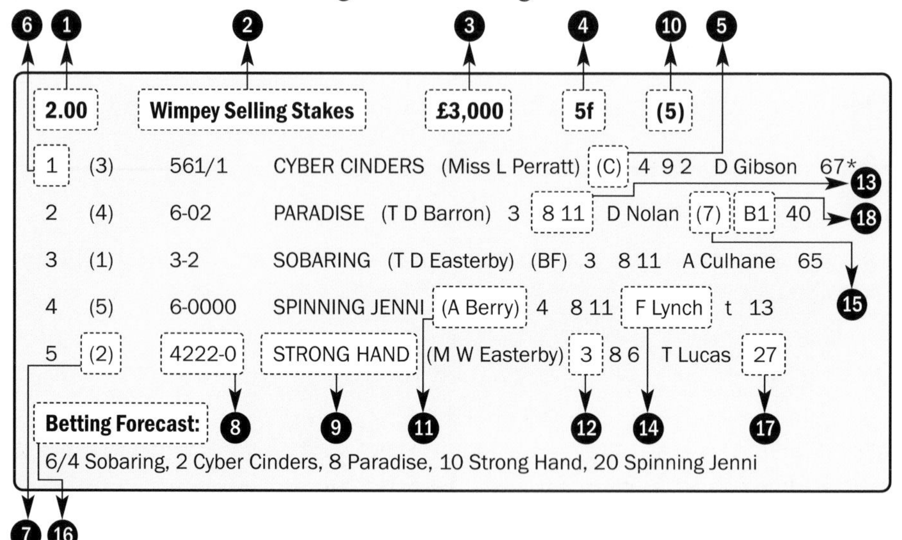

KEY

1. Time of race.
2. Name of race.
3. Prize money to be allocated to winning owners.
4. Distance of race (5f means five furlongs, the minimum race distance in the UK. This equates to 5/8 of a mile, or 1000 metres. One furlong = 200 metres).
5. Form record. D = distance winner (there are no horses in this race that have won over five furlongs), C = course winner (Cyber Cinders has won at this track), and BF = beaten favourite (Sobaring was beaten when favourite last time out).
6. Race card number. These are allocated at the overnight declaration stage and should be referred to when betting verbally with bookmakers.
7. Draw position (Flat racing only).
8. Form of the horse's most recent performances. '-' indicates the previous season's form, and '/' shows form from more than two seasons prior to today's race.
9. Name of the horse.
10. Number of declared runners.
11. Name of the trainer.
12. Age of the horse.
13. Weight the horse should carry today. 8 11 means the horse will carry 8 stones and 11 pounds in weight.
14. Name of the jockey.
15. Jockey's allowance (if apprentice, amateur etc.).
16. Betting forecast.
17. Rating devised by the newspaper's individual expert. The higher the rating, the better chance the horse has in their opinion.
18. Declaration of any headgear or extra equipment that the horse will carry. The most common forms are: B = blinkers, V = visor, T = tongue strap, E/S = eye shield; P = cheekpieces; H = hood. When '1' appears after the nominated piece of equipment, it signifies that the horse will be sporting the equipment for the first time.

Handicap Races Explained

Just like human athletes, there are many racehorses with a natural talent for being faster than others. If the fastest racehorses were allowed to enter any race then they would keep winning at ridiculously short odds. Racing has a method of preventing this by giving every horse that has raced three or more times the option of receiving a rating. Handicap ratings are provided by a team employed by the British Horseracing Authority, each with their own specialist division, e.g. two-year-olds, or sprinters, for instance.

Frankel ended his illustrious career with an official rating of 140, the highest rating ever given to a Flat horse, whereas a more moderate racehorse may finish their career with a rating of less than 50.

On the Flat, there are six classes of race, with Class 1 races run for the equine elite, and Class 6 races for less gifted horses. The more a horse runs, the more exposed the horse becomes to the handicapper, so he can rate the horse more accurately on the variety of form that he has shown. The handicapper may, at his discretion, discount a performance if the horse had proved that he doesn't handle either very soft or firm ground, for instance.

There is no particular science involved, it's merely an experienced opinion created by someone that watches thousands of races every year. As the rating is based on opinion, it is not completely flawless, but errors made by the handicapper are generally only marginal. However, the difference between winning and losing a fortune can be just a matter of millimetres.

In handicaps, each rating figure relates to the weight that the horse will carry. The jockey must weigh in and out before and after a race, to ensure that he and his saddle make the allotted weight, according to the conditions of the race.

There are different sets of official ratings for Flat (turf), Flat (all-weather), over hurdles and over steeplechase fences. Usually, horses must race three times before a rating can be allocated. Ratings may also be allocated to horses who have run just once or twice, as long as they have won a race. Once awarded a rating, each rating point equates to 1lb in weight for handicap race purposes.

For example, a race could have a rating span of 50-70 and may have a top weight of 10 stone. Any horse with an official BHA rating of 71 or greater would not qualify to be entered into the race. The horse rated 70 in this example, would carry 10st exactly, and a horse rated 65 would carry 9st 9lb, and so on.

The idea is that a handicap race will give lesser-rated horses a better chance against more able horses, because they are burdened with less weight to carry. Races are structured within rating spans, to ensure that have a similar rating are forced to compete together, to prevent lesser horses from carrying more weight than they should, as the margin between top and bottom weight is never less than 28lb. Races are generally framed in groups, for instance 56-70, 76-80 etc. This helps prevent a 'long handicap' from forming (see 'Glossary').

If you can find a horse that is AHEAD OF THE HANDICAPPER, you are likely to have found a good value bet. In other words, the rating that the BHA handicapper has allocated needs to be lower than the rating you think the horse should have, based on your analysis of its previous form. Official ratings can be found in The Racing Post, along with the form of every horse running on any given day.

Handicappers rate horses by taking one horse in each race as a benchmark. They will have decided that this particular horse has run its typical race, and that it has run to its handicap mark. Horses that finished either in front or behind will then be rated according to how far they have been beaten or have beaten said horse. The weight they have received/conceded is also taken into account. It is possible for you to do the same. You must also take into account whether each horse likes the ground, or whether they were effective over the distance. E.g. the form cannot be interpreted literally if the horse failed to stay, or needed further. This requires hours of research, but could be profitable if you display good judgement. The Racing Post publishes its own rating and a 'Topspeed' rating, which can be taken into account when making selections. These are usually compared in the form summary.

One winner-finding concept is to select horses that have run up to four times. These horses could be unexposed, so may have a decent win within their capability. It pays to watch as much racing as possible, so that you can make a note of any horses that have run well recently, without exposing themselves too much. This may include horses that have met with trouble in running, which may have gone unnoticed, or horses that have won a small race, but look as though they could cope with a step up in trip or grade.

A basic guide to handicapping:

FLAT	
5f	3lb per length
6f	2.5lb per length
7f-8f	2lb per length
9-10f	1.75lb per length
11-13f	1.5lb per length
14f	1.25lb per length
15f+	1lb per length

JUMPS
1lb per length is used in most instances except over very long distances or on very testing ground. Any pound carried over 12st (likely in Hunter Chases and with horses carrying penalties) is worth 2 lengths.

Frankel - Rated 140 at the end of his career

The Zeton System

This system selects sixteen Flat racing trainers and nine National Hunt trainers. The full details can be found in the following pages (17 to 41).

Each map has a shaded area and a non-shaded area.

When the trainer has a horse running at a racecourse within the non-shaded area (or outside of Great Britain and the Republic of Ireland) in a race with total prize money of £10,000 or less, your bet is on. Win-only (if odds are less than 5-1) or each-way bet (if the odds are 5-1 or greater).

The location of British Racecourses can be found on page 92.

The theory behind this system is that particular high-profile trainers may think twice before going to the time, effort and expense of sending a horse from their training yards to racecourses that are a considerable distance away, particularly when the race prize money at stake is not substantial.

When races do have substantial prize money, the trainer is likely to consider place prize money to be worthwhile, which isn't really overly positive as a potential winning indicator and is why these races are ignored in the Zeton System. Furthermore, where the race is Group 1 (Flat) or Grade 1 (National Hunt) the trainer may be angling to settle for a place to gain black type (see page 148). Hence the reason why this system ignores races with total prize money in excess of £10,000.

Charlie Appleby

Moulton Paddocks, Newmarket

Raised in Plymouth by parents who raced Arabian horses, Charlie soon ventured to Newmarket once he realised he was too big to be a jockey. He joined Susan Piggott, staying there until she retired from training in the mid-nineties. He then moved to work for trainer David Loder, who was enjoying an incredible run of form at the time, with Sheikh Mohammed as his biggest patron. Eventually, he moved with Loder when he was set up as a private trainer to Sheikh Mohammed at the defunct Evry Racecourse in France. During this time, Charlie was spending each winter in Dubai breaking in yearlings and two-year-olds. When David Loder returned to Newmarket to become a public trainer after just two years in France, Charlie remained in Dubai working for the Sheikh. He travelled horses all around the world until eventually settling at Moulton Paddocks in Newmarket assisting new Godolphin trainer Mahmood Al Zarooni. Controversially, Al Zarooni was later warned off for administering steroids to his horses, which led to Charlie taking over the licence in July 2013. In his first season, Outstrip represented the stable in all the top two-year-old races, eventually winning the Breeders' Cup Juvenile at Santa Anita. He trained over a hundred winners the following year and looks set to be a constant major force.

Most Notable Winners

Charming Thought
2014 Middle Park Stakes, Newmarket.

Outstrip
2013 Breeders' Cup Juvenile, Santa Anita.

Sudden Wonder
2014 £200,000 Tattersalls Millions Two-year-old Trophy, Newmarket.

Wedding Ring
2013 £300,000 Tattersalls Millions Two-year-old Fillies' Trophy, Newmarket.

Andrew Balding

Park House Stables, Kingsclere

In 2003, Andrew Balding took over the licence from his father, Ian, who had enjoyed an illustrious training career at Kingsclere, handling champions such as Mill Reef and Lochsong. Andrew returned home after spells as an amateur jockey with his uncle, Toby Balding, and as assistant to Northern trainer Lynda Ramsden. Toby Balding was the first trainer to employ Tony McCoy when he first came from Ireland, helping him to win the conditional jockeys' title. Toby was a great mentor to so many, including Andrew in his youth. In his first season, he trained Casual Look to win the Epsom Oaks, followed by a very emotional interview with his sister, Clare, the very well respected sport broadcaster. Since then, Andrew has been one of the most successful Flat trainers in the country, passing the 100-winner mark for the first time in 2013. Never afraid to send horses overseas, he has profited from huge international prizes with Side Glance and Phoenix Reach. He has also been instrumental in the careers of young jockeys David Probert and Oisin Murphy, the champion apprentice of 2014.

Most Notable Winners

Bonfire
2012 Dante Stakes, York.

Casual Look
2003 Oaks, Epsom.

Dream Eater
2007 £300,000 St Leger Two-year-old Stakes, Doncaster.

Elm Park
2014 Royal Lodge Stakes, Ascot.
2014 Racing Post Trophy, Doncaster.

I Love Me
2010 £200,000 Tattersalls Millions Auction Trophy, Newmarket.

Phoenix Reach
2004 Hong Kong Vase, Sha Tin.
2004 Canadian International, Woodbine.
2005 Dubai Sheema Classic, Nad Al Sheba.

Side Glance
2013 Longines Mackinnon Stakes, Flemington.

Saeed Bin Suroor

Godolphin Stables, Newmarket,
and Al Quoz Stables, Dubai

Saeed bin Suroor is Godolphin's longest-serving trainer, having established himself in Newmarket at the start of the 1995 season. Whilst still a policeman in his native Dubai, with an interest in training horses as a hobby, he was head-hunted by Sheikh Mohammed, who sent him 30 horses to test his skills. The Sheikh was happy with the results, so employed him as a private trainer at Godolphin Stables at Newmarket, with immediate success. The unbeaten Lammtarra made a timely advertisement for his skill as a trainer by winning the Derby, the King George and the Arc after suffering from a bout of colic prior to his Epsom win. Moonshell had won the Oaks the day before, and Classic Cliche went on to win the St Leger, all in his first season. Saeed has been champion trainer four times, and has helped Godolphin to win nine owners' titles. Saeed has also enjoyed an incredible seven wins in the world's richest race, the Dubai World Cup.

Most Notable Recent Winners

African Story
2014 Dubai World Cup, Meydan.

Farhh
2013 Lockinge Stakes, Newbury.
2013 Champion Stakes, Ascot.

Hunter's Light
2015 Jebel Hatta, Meydan.

Prince Bishop
2015 Dubai World Cup, Meydan.

Sajjhaa
2013 Dubai Duty Free, Meydan.

Vale Of York
2010 Breeders' Cup Juvenile, Santa Anita.

Jim Bolger

Coolcullen, Co. Kilkenny

The master of Coolcullen is a great producer of great horses, jockeys and trainers. Champions Willie Mullins, Aidan O'Brien, Tony McCoy, and Paul Carberry all began their careers with Jim Bolger, who is renowned for playing his cards very close to his chest. He is a prolific horse-breeder as well as a trainer, and sells many of his homebreds after they have performed on the racecourse, often for a substantial profit. In recent times, both New Approach and his son Dawn Approach were bred and owned by the trainer before being sold to Godolphin. Jim Bolger gains assistance from his son-in-law, Kevin Manning, who rides the majority of the stable's runners.

Most Notable Recent Winners

Dawn Approach
2012 Dewhurst Stakes, Newmarket.
2013 2,000 Guineas, Newmarket.
2013 St James Palace Stakes, Royal Ascot.

Finsceal Beo
2006 Prix Marcel Boussac, Longchamp.
2007 Irish 1,000 Guineas, The Curragh.

Lush Lashes
2008 Coronation Stakes, Royal Ascot.
2008 Matron Stakes, Leopardstown.

New Approach
2008 Derby, Epsom.
2008 Irish Champion Stakes, Leopardstown.
2008 Champion Stakes, Ascot.

Parish Hall
2011 Dewhurst Stakes, Newmarket.

Pleascach
2015 Yorkshire Oaks, York.
2015 Irish 1,000 Gunieas, The Curragh.

Trading Leather
2013 Irish Derby, The Curragh.

Roger Charlton

Beckhampton House Stables, Wiltshire

Roger first went to Beckhampton Stables in 1978 to assist the renowned trainer, Jeremy Tree. Beckhampton is the most fabulous training establishment, having been resident to fellow greats Fred and Sam Darling, and Sir Noel Murless, before he moved to Warren Place in Newmarket. In his brief riding career, Roger won the Kim Muir Chase at the Cheltenham Festival, beating the great amateur Hon. John Lawrence (Lord Oaksey), in the process. Roger began training in 1990, upon the retirement of his former employer. He enjoyed immediate success with two Group 1 winners in his first summer, with Sanglamore winning the Prix Du Jockey Club, and just three days later Quest For Fame won the Epsom Derby. Roger has also enjoyed Group 1 success with Thistle Bird, Tamarisk, Patavellian, Tante Rose, Avonbridge, Cityscape, and Al Kazeem. Perhaps one of Roger's greatest training accomplishments was bringing Al Kazeem back from his failed stud career to finish second in the Champion Stakes and win the Prix d'Harcourt at Longchamp.

Most Notable Recent Winners

Al Kazeem
2013 Eclipse Stakes, Sandown.
2013 Prince Of Wale's Stakes, Royal Ascot.
2013 Tattersalls Gold Cup, The Curragh.
2015 Tattersalls Gold Cup, The Curragh.

Avonbridge
2005 Prix de l'Abbaye, Longchamp.

Cityscape
2012 Dubai Duty Free, Meydan.

Patavellian
2003 Prix de l'Abbaye, Longchamp.

Thistle Bird
2014 Pretty Polly Stakes, Newmarket.

Luca Cumani

Bedford House Stables, Newmarket

Luca was born in Milan in 1949, to mother Elena, who was a champion amateur jockey, and father Sergio, a champion trainer in their native Italy. Luca came to England to assist Sir Henry Cecil before taking out his licence in 1976 at Bedford House Stables in Newmarket, where he trains to this day.

Luca has twice won the Epsom Derby, with Kahyasi and High Rise, as well as training winners all around the world. Luca has plundered valuable prizes with Falbrav (Hong Kong Cup and the Prix D'Ispahan), Starcraft (Prix du Moulin) and Alkaased (Japan Cup, Grand Prix de Saint Cloud). Barathea was a superb winner of the Breeders' Cup Mile in 1994 under a fresh-faced Frankie Dettori, long before it was common for European horses to travel to the US. Luca has also been a mentor to many remarkable jockeys, most notably Frankie Dettori, Jimmy Fortune and Jason Weaver.

Most Notable Recent Winners

Afsare
2013 Celebration Mile, Goodwood.

Alkaased
2005 Japan Cup, Sha Tin,
2005 Grand Prix de St Cloud, St Cloud.

Falbrav
2003 Eclipse Stakes, Sandown,
2003 International Stakes, York,
2003 Queen Elizabeth II Stakes, Ascot &
2003 Hong Kong Cup, Sha Tin.

Postponed
2015 King George VI, Ascot.
2015 Queen Elizabeth Stakes, Ascot.

Second Step
2015 Grosser Preis Von Berlin, Hoppegarten.

Starcraft
2005 Queen Elizabeth II Stakes, Ascot &
2005 Prix du Moulin, Longchamp.

Gordon Elliott

Cullentra House, Co. Meath

Hailing from a non-racing background, Gordon made an immediate impact on the racing world by becoming the youngest trainer ever to win a Grand National, in only his second season. In fact, in the post-race interview, presenter Clare Balding didn't even know his first name! He began his career in racing as an amateur jockey to both Tony Martin and Martin Pipe, but it was always training that interested him. When Silver Birch recorded his Aintree success, Gordon still hadn't even trained a winner in Ireland. Since then, Gordon has recorded hundreds of winners, including many in Britain, where he is the leading trainer at Perth by a decent margin. The Elliott string is now respected at the highest level of National Hunt racing.

Most Notable Winners

Bayan
2015 Ladbroke Handicap Hurdle, Ascot.

Cause Of Causes
2015 National Hunt Chase, Cheltenham.

Clarcam
2014 Racing Post Novices' Chase, Leopardstown.

Don Cossack
2014 John Durkan Memorial Chase, Punchestown.
2015 Melling Chase, Aintree.
2015 Punchestown Gold Cup, Punchestown.

Roi Du Mee
2013 J N Wine Champion Chase, Down Royal.

Tiger Roll
2014 Triumph Hurdle, Cheltenham.

Richard Fahey

Mews House, Musley Bank, Malton

Richard Fahey began his racing career as a jockey, riding over a hundred winners, before embarking on his training career. Each year since he started in the early 1990s, results have been on an upward curve, making him one of the most prolific trainers in the country. 2014 was his best season yet, with nearly £3 million in prize-money won, and a fourth-place finish in the trainers' table. Good horses, such as Superior Premium, helped to raise the yard's profile back in the '90s, and have since been followed by a steady stream of pattern-race winners. Wootton Bassett finished the 2010 season as champion two-year-old in France after winning the Prix Jean-Luc Lagadere, and now stands there as a stallion. Fahey has also trained winners in Ireland and Dubai, and is a force to be reckoned with anywhere he has runners.

Most Notable Winners

Baccarat
2014 Wokingham Stakes, Royal Ascot.

Bond's Girl
2014 Weatherbys Insurance 2yo Stakes, Doncaster.

Don't Touch
2015 Ayr Gold Cup.

Gabrial
2015 Lincoln Handicap, Doncaster.

Garswood
2013 Lennox Sprint Stakes, Goodwood.
2014 Prix Maurice de Gheest, Deauville.

Mayson
2012 July Cup, Newmarket.
2012 Palace House Stakes, Newmarket.

Mr Lupton
2015 Weatherbys £300,000 2yo Stakes, Doncaster.

Wootton Bassett
2010 DBS Premier Yearling Stakes, York,
2010 £300,000 2yo Stakes, Doncaster.
2010 Prix Jean-Luc Lagadere, Longchamp.

James Fanshawe

Pegasus Stables, Newmarket

After working as assistant trainer to Sir Michael Stoute, James Fanshawe began training at the historic Pegasus Stables in Newmarket in 1990. Starting out with 32 horses, James was well supported by Sir Michael, who encouraged his owners to place horses at Pegasus Stables. James's first winner as a trainer was Black Sapphire, owned by Sheikh Mohammed. Since then, he has enjoyed many high-profile victories, including five Group 1 wins with Elite Racing Club's Soviet Song, plus Group 1 wins with Ribbons, Seal Of Approval and Frizzante. He enjoyed a big-race double at Royal Ascot in 2011, with Society Rock winning the Golden Jubilee Stakes and Deacon Blues winning the Wokingham Handicap. James has also trained two Champion Hurdle winners, Royal Gait and Hors La Loi III, proving James's versatility as a trainer.

Most Notable Recent Winners

Frizzante
2004 July Cup, Newmarket.

High Jinx
2014 Prix du Cadran, Longchamp.

Ribbons
2014 Prix Jean Romanet, Deauville.

Seal Of Approval
2013 British Champions Fillies & Mares Stakes, Ascot.

Society Rock
2005 Falmouth Stakes, Newmarket.
2005 Sprint Cup, Haydock.

Soviet Song
2002 Fillies' Mile, Ascot.
2004 Sussex Stakes, Goodwood.
2004 Ridgewood Pearl Stakes, Leopardstown.
2004/5 Falmouth Stakes, Newmarket.

Zidane
2007 Stewards Cup, Goodwood.

John Gosden

Clarehaven Stables, Newmarket

After graduating from Cambridge University, John joined the renowned trainer Sir Noel Murless as an assistant, before moving to the previous master of Ballydoyle, Vincent O'Brien. He then moved to California to assist Tommy Doyle, before taking out a licence for himself a year later, after a remarkable 500 winners in the US. This included a Breeders' Cup winner and two of his horses winning Eclipse Awards. John returned to Newmarket in 1989 and has since trained over 2,000 winners in Britain and Europe. He has conquered nearly every feature race, including the Derby (Benny The Dip), the King George (Taghrooda), the 1,000 Guineas (Lahan) as well as four St Legers. Recently, Gosden trained Khalid Abdullah's homebred Kingman to win the Irish 2,000 Guineas, the St James's Palace Stakes, the Sussex Stakes and the Prix Jacques le Marois, earning him the coveted title of Horse of the Year. John trained Oasis Dream for many top-level sprint victories, with the horse now featuring among the top stallions in the world.

Most Notable Recent Winners

Kingman
2014 Irish 1,000 Guineas, The Curragh.
2014 St James Palace Stakes, Royal Ascot.
2014 Sussex Stakes, Goodwood.
2014 Prix Jacques le Marois, Deauville.

Taghrooda
2014 Oaks, Epsom, 2014 King George VI and Queen Elizabeth Diamond Stakes, Ascot.

Golden Horn
2015 Derby, Epsom.
2015 Eclipse Stakes, Sandown.
2015 Irish Champions Stakes, Leopardstown.

Jack Hobbs
2015 Irish Derby, The Curragh.

Shalaa
2015 Prix Morny, Deauville.
2015 Middle Park Stakes, Newmarket.

Star Of Seville
2015 Prix de Diane, Chantilly.

Sultania
2014 Nassau Stakes, Goodwood.

William Haggas

Somerville Lodge Stables, Newmarket

William Haggas is based in Newmarket and is the son-in-law of the legendary Lester Piggott. He started working in his father's textile factory after leaving school, before entering the horseracing industry. He moved to Newmarket to assist John Winter and renowned mentor Sir Mark Prescott before taking his own licence out in 1987. His biggest winners have come with Shaamit in the 1996 Epsom Derby, and Dancing Rain, winner of the 2011 Epsom and German Oaks. William has enjoyed his most successful seasons in 2013 and 2014, training over 100 winners in both seasons. He enjoys a consistent supply of quality horses from Sheikh Hamdan and is respected as one of the most powerful stables in the country.

Most Notable Recent Winners

Aqlaam
2009 Prix du Moulin, Longchamp.

Dancing Rain
2011 Oaks, Epsom.
2011 Preis der Diana - Deutsches Stuten-Derby, Dusseldorf.

Fury
2010 £500,000 Tattersalls Millions 2yo Trophy, Newmarket.

Haikbidiac
2013 DBS Premiere Yearling Stakes, Doncaster.

King's Apostle
2009 Prix Maurice de Gheest, Deauville.

Mukhadram
2014 Eclipse Stakes, Sandown.

Richard Hannon

Herridge and Everleigh Stables, Wiltshire

Richard Hannon (junior) has been at the helm of his father's all conquering stable for years before taking over the reins at the start of the 2014 season. His father was champion trainer five times and trained nearly 4000 winners, including 35 Group 1s, and is immortalised in racing folklore. Richard jnr made an immediate impact to his training career when winning the 2,000 Guineas with Night Of Thunder, the only horse to beat Kingman in the latter's glittering career. Olympic Glory soon added to the headlines when winning the Lockinge Stakes later that month. Richard also handled the Cartier Award-winning juvenile, Tiggy Wiggy, winner of the Weatherbys Super Sprint, the Lowther and the Cheveley Park Stakes, who substantially contributed to the total of 23 Group winners in the trainer's rookie season.

Most Notable Winners

Olympic Glory
2014 Lockinge Stakes, Newbury.
2014 Prix de la Foret, Longchamp.

Night Of Thunder
2014 2,000 Guineas, Newmarket.
2015 Lockinge Stakes, Newbury.

Pethers Moon
2015 Coronation Cup, Epsom.

Tiggy Wiggy
2014 Cheveley Park Stakes, Newmarket.

Toronado
2014 Queen Anne Stakes, Royal Ascot.

Nicky Henderson

Seven Barrows, Lambourn

Nicky Henderson has been at the forefront of the sport for the last three decades. Nicky's father, Johnny, was instrumental in setting up the Racecourse Holdings Trust, which saved Cheltenham racecourse from property developers in the 1960s. Nicky entered the sport as an amateur rider, winning the Imperial Cup and Aintree's Foxhunters' Chase, and later became Fred Winter's assistant trainer. Taking out his own licence in 1978, Nicky quickly rose through the ranks to become champion jumps trainer twice between 1985 and 1987, winning three Champion Hurdles in this period with See You Then. Nicky moved out of the centre of Lambourn to Seven Barrows in 1992 and quickly built the yard into one of the most powerful in the country. Numerous Grade 1 winners came from the yard, including Remittance Man, winner of the Arkle, Champion Chase and Melling Chase, as well as Marlborough, Tiutchev and Landing Light. The last few years have seen Nicky mount a strong challenge to the dominance of all conquering trainer, Paul Nicholls. In 2012, Nicky trained seven winners at Cheltenham and six Aintree winners, including the remarkable Sprinter Sacre, who remained unbeaten that season and had encouraged comparisons with Arkle. These successes helped Nicky to clinch a third trainer's title in the 2012/13 season.

Most Notable Recent Winners

Bobs Worth
2012 RSA Chase, Cheltenham.
2012 Hennessy Gold Cup, Newbury.
2013 Gold Cup, Cheltenham.
2013 Lexus Chase, Leopardstown.

Finian's Rainbow
2012 Queen Mother Champion Chase, Cheltenham.

L'Ami Serge
2015 Tolworth Hurdle, Sandown.

Peace And Co
2015 Triumph Hurdle, Cheltenham.

Riverside Theatre
2012 Ryanair Chase, Cheltenham.

Sprinter Sacre
2012 Arkle Chase, Cheltenham.
2012 Tingle Creek Chase, Sandown.
2013 Champion Chase, Cheltenham.
2013 Melling Chase, Aintree.
2013 Champion Chase, Punchestown.

Whisper
2015 Silver Cross Stayers' Hurdle, Aintree.

Charles Hills

Faringdon Place, Lambourn

Charles Hills took over the licence from his father Barry in 2011 after eight years spent as assistant at Faringdon Place in Lambourn. He had previously gained experience working for the Hayes family in Australia and had enjoyed two years assisting James Fanshawe in Newmarket. Two years after taking over the yard, he landed his first Classic when Just The Judge obliged in the 1,000 Guineas at The Curragh. The following year, the ill-fated Chriselliam landed the Juvenile Fillies' Turf race at the Breeders' Cup, and Just The Judge returned to form to win the valuable E. P. Taylor Stakes at Woodbine that winter. Charles has a steady supply of horses from Sheikh Hamdan and other leading owners, which make his yard very powerful every season.

Most Notable Winners

Chriselliam

2013 Fillies' Mile, Ascot.
2013 Breeders' Cup Juvenile Fillies' Turf, Santa Anita.

Just The Judge

2012 Rockfel Stakes, Newmarket.
2013 Irish 1,000 Guineas, The Curragh.
2014 E. P. Taylor Stakes, Woodbine.

Magical Memory

2015 Stewards Cup, Goodwood.

Muhaarar

2014 Gimcrack Stakes, York.
2015 Greenham Stakes, Newbury.
2015 Commonwealth Cup, Ascot.
2015 July Cup, Newmarket.
2015 Prix Maurice de Gheest, Deauville.

Philip Hobbs

Billbrook Stables, Minehead

Philip was raised around horses, his father being a farmer and permit-holder, and having sent out some decent winners in the family colours. After attending Reading University, he rode in point-to-points and showjumped to a high level before becoming a professional jockey at the age of 21. Philip rode 160 winners in a ten-year career before starting his training yard in the early eighties, helped by his wife Sarah, daughter of Bertie Hill, an equestrian Olympic gold medalist. Philip has now trained over 2,000 winners, meaning his Minehead yard is always in the top six Jumps yards each season. Philip provides jockey Richard Johnson with the majority of his firepower. They have enjoyed great success with the likes of Rooster Booster, Balthazar King, Fair Along, Monkerhostin, Wishfull Thinking and Flagship Uberalles. They have also enjoyed the odd high-profile Flat success over the years in stayers' handicaps, such as the Cesarewitch and Northumberland Plate.

Most Notable Recent Winners

Captain Chris
2011 Arkle Chase, Cheltenham.
2014 Betfair Ascot Chase, Ascot.

Detroit City
2006 Triumph Hurdle, Cheltenham.
2006 Cesarewitch Handicap, Newmarket.

Made In Japan
2004 Triumph Hurdle, Cheltenham.

Massini's Maguire
2007 Ballymore Properties Novices' Hurdle, Cheltenham.

Menorah
2010 Supreme Novices' Hurdle, Cheltenham.
2012 Manifesto Novices' Chase, Aintree.

One Knight
2004 RSA Chase, Cheltenham.

Rooster Booster
2003 Champion Hurdle, Cheltenham.

Unleash
2003 Northumberland Plate, Newcastle.

Mark Johnston

Kingsley House Stables, Middleham

Scottish trainer, Mark Johnston has trained, on average, over two hundred winners per year during the last decade. After leaving school, he became a qualified vet, and spent three years practising after graduating. He began training in Lincolnshire in the late eighties, before purchasing Kingsley House, Middleham, a year later. Mark added two more yards around the North Yorkshire town and the stable has since become a serious stronghold. In 1994 he trained a hundred winners for the first time and has not looked back. He has trained the winners of the 1,000 and 2,000 Guineas, three Ascot Gold Cups and five Goodwood Cups, as well as over 3,000 winners. He regularly trains over 200 winners per season and has handled the likes of Attraction, Mister Baileys, Royal Rebel, Double Trigger, Shamardal and Jukebox Jury.

Most Notable Recent Winners

Awzaan
2009 Middle Park Stakes, Newmarket.

Bow Creek
2014 Boomerang Mile, Leopardstown.
2014 Celebration Mile, Goodwood.

Buratino
2015 Coventry Stakes, Royal Ascot.

Jukebox Jury
2009 Grand Prix de Deauville, Deauville.
2009 Prix Von Europa, Cologne.
2011 Irish St Leger, The Curragh.

Kirklees
2006 Gran Criterium, San Siro

Lumiere
2015 Cheveley Park Stakes, Newmarket.

Scatter Dice
2013 Cesarewitch, Newmarket.

Secret Brief
2014 £500,000 Tattersalls Millions 2yo Trophy, Newmarket.

Alan King

Barbury Castle, Wiltshire

Alan King developed a passion for racing from a young age, beginning his career as a teenager with one of Britain's greatest National Hunt trainers, David Nicholson, near Cheltenham. Alan went on to become assistant to 'The Duke' and held that position until Nicholson retired 15 years later. After taking over the licence mid-season, Alan accomplished an exceptional tally of 31 winners within six months, which included victory in the Grade 1 Long Walk Hurdle at Ascot with Anzum. In the summer of 2000, he moved to the stunning Barbury Castle in Wiltshire and has since enjoyed plenty of high-profile winners, including Elite Racing Club's Penzance, in the Triumph Hurdle. He also trained Katchit to win both the Triumph Hurdle and the Champion Hurdle the following year, as well winning with star horses Voy Por Ustedes and My Way De Solzen, who won the remarkable combination of the World Hurdle and the Arkle.

Most Notable Recent Winners

Balder Success
2014 Maghull Novices' Chase, Ascot.
2015 Ascot Chase, Ascot.

Blazing Bailey
2008 World Series Hurdle, Punchestown.

Godsmejudge
2013 Scottish Grand National, Ayr.

Katchit
2007 Triumph Hurdle, Cheltenham.
2008 Champion Hurdle, Cheltenham.

My Way De Solzen
2006 World Hurdle, Cheltenham.
2007 Arkle Chase, Cheltenham.

Voy Por Ustedes
2009 Melling Chase, Aintree.
2007 Champion Chase, Cheltenham.

Uxizandre
2014 Manifesto Novices' Chase, Aintree.
2015 Ryanair Chase, Cheltenham.

Donald McCain

Bankhouse, Cheshire

Donald is the son of Aintree legend 'Ginger' McCain, best known for training the only triple Grand National winner, Red Rum, from behind his car showroom in Southport. Donald has therefore been immersed in the racing industry his entire life, and left for Newmarket as soon as he finished school, going to work for Luca Cumani for a couple of years. From Newmarket, Donald went to Lambourn, joining Oliver Sherwood as pupil assistant and stable amateur. Donald followed in his father's footsteps when taking over the training at Bankhouse in 2006. Donald is nearing 1,000 winners, including victories at the Cheltenham Festival, the Scottish Champion Hurdle, the Galway Hurdle and the Ascot Hurdle. The highlight of his training career to date is Ballabriggs' Aintree Grand National win in 2011.

Most Notable Recent Winners

Ballabriggs
2011 Grand National, Aintree.

Cinders and Ashes
2012 Supreme Novices' Hurdle, Cheltenham.

Hollow Tree
2011 Finale Juvenile Hurdle, Chepstow.

Overturn
2010 Northumberland Plate, Newcastle.
2010 Galway Hurdle, Galway.
2011 Chester Cup, Chester.
2011 Fighting Fifth Hurdle, Newcastle.

Peddlers Cross
2010 Fighting Fifth Hurdle, Newbury.
2010 Neptune Novices' Hurdle, Cheltenham.

Willie Mullins

Closesutton, Co. Carlow

Willie Mullins was the champion amateur jockey in Ireland for six seasons prior to joining Jim Bolger as an assistant trainer. He had previously assisted his father, Paddy, who was the champion trainer in Ireland ten times himself, as well as training the brilliant mare Dawn Run to win both the Champion Hurdle and the Gold Cup, and remains the only horse ever to do so. Since then, Willie has become a trainer in his own right, and his stable has gone from strength to strength, having won nearly every major prize in Britain, Ireland and France. Heavily supported by renowned American owner, Rich Ricci, the stable trained a record-breaking eight winners at the 2015 Cheltenham Festival, including finishing first, second and third in the Champion Hurdle. Even more remarkable was his 16 winners at Punchestown the following month. With his current string of horses, it is difficult to see how Mullins can be challenged in most of the feature races in Ireland and many others in Europe to boot.

Most Notable Recent Winners

Annie Power
2015 Mares' Champion Hurdle, Punchestown.

Douvan
2015 Supreme Novices' Hurdle, Cheltenham.

Faugheen
2014 Neptune Novices' Hurdle, Cheltenham.
2014 Christmas Hurdle, Kempton.
2015 Champion Hurdle, Cheltenham.
2015 Champion Hurdle, Punchestown.

Hurricane Fly
2011, 2013 Champion Hurdle, Cheltenham, 2011, 2012, 2013, 2014, 2015 Irish Champion Hurdle, Leopardstown, 2010, 2012, 2013, 2014 Festival Hurdle, Leopardstown, 2010 & 2011, 2012, 2013 Champion Hurdle, Punchestown.

Quevega
2009, 2010, 2011, 2012, 2013, 2014 David Nicholson Mares' Hurdle, Cheltenham.

Un De Sceaux
2015 Arkle Chase, Leopardstown.
2015 Arkle Chase, Cheltenham.
2015 Ryanair Novices' Chase, Punchestown.

Vautour
2014 Supreme Novices' Hurdle, Cheltenham.
2015 JLT Novices' Chase, Cheltenham.

Paul Nicholls

Ditcheat, Somerset

Paul Nicholls was born in Gloucester in 1962 to a family with no particular racing background. He left school at 16 and joined local point-to-point trainer, Dick Baimbridge, one of the most prolific men in the sport. Paul began riding in point-to-points and then progressed under Rules, joining trainer David Barons, and rode over a hundred winners. After being kicked by a horse and breaking his leg, Paul remained with Barons for two years as an assistant, before setting up for himself in Ditcheat in 1991. His first major winner came two years later when the ill-fated See More Indians won the Feltham Chase at Kempton on Boxing Day, and he did not have to wait long for See More Business to raise the yard's profile further by winning the 1997 King George VI Chase. Paul has remained champion trainer since the retirement of Martin Pipe every season bar one, and trained the remarkable trio of Kauto Star, Denman and Big Buck's in the same era. His current stable stars include Silviniaco Conti and Saphir Du Rheu.

Most Notable Recent Winners

All Yours
2015 Anniversary 4yo Hurdle, Aintree.

Big Buck's
2010, 2011, 2012, 2013 World Hurdle, Cheltenham.
2010, 2011, 2012, 2013 Liverpool Hurdle, Aintree.

Dodging Bullets
2014 Tingle Creek Chase, Sandown.
2015 Champion Chase, Cheltenham.
2015 Clarence House Chase, Ascot.

Irving
2014 Fighting Fifth Hurdle, Newcastle.

Neptune Collonges
2012 Grand National, Aintree.

Saphir Du Rheu
2015 Mildmay Novices' Chase, Aintree.

Silviniaco Conti
2013, 2014 King George VI Chase, Kempton.
2013, 2014 Betfred Bowl, Aintree.
2012, 2014 Betfair Chase, Haydock.

Vibrato Valtat
2014 Henry VIII Chase, Sandown.

Aidan O'Brien

Ballydoyle, Co. Tipperary

Aidan O'Brien set out to follow in the footsteps of his namesake, the former Master of Ballydoyle, Vincent O'Brien, from an early stage. In the same year that Aidan was crowned champion amateur jockey of Ireland, he trained a winner on the first day he had a runner. In 2001, he became the youngest trainer ever to win a British trainers' championship, and only the second overseas trainer to do so, the other being his predecessor, Vincent O'Brien. Since then, he has trained countless Group 1 winners, mainly supplied by the Coolmore Racing dynasty, headed by John Magnier. He has enjoyed over fifty Classic winners alone in Britain and Ireland, and is guaranteed an even flow of new superstars with the finest pedigrees sourced from around the world. Once Aidan's best horses retire, they tend to progress to Coolmore to stand at stud or to be covered, the best example being world champion sire, Galileo. Aidan trains at Ballydoyle, which has facilities cultivated by Vincent over sixty years ago, boasting the best surfaces and gradients for horses to be trained in the world to prepare them for competing at the highest level.

Most Notable Recent Winners

Air Force Blue
2015 National Stakes, The Curragh.
2015 Phoenix Stakes, The Curragh.

Australia
2014 Derby, Epsom, 2014 Irish Derby, The Curragh & 2014 International Stakes, York.

Gleneagles
2015 2,000 Guineas, Newmarket.
2015 St. James's Palace Stakes, Ascot.
2015 Irish 2,000 Guineas, The Curragh.

Magician
2013 2,000 Guineas & 2013 Breeders' Cup Turf, Santa Anita.

Minding
2015 Moyglare Stud Stakes, The Curragh.

Order Of St George
2015 Irish St Leger, The Curragh.

Qualify
2015 Oaks, Epsom.

St Nicholas Abbey
2009 Racing Post Trophy, Doncaster, 2011.
2011, 2012, 2013 Coronation Cup, Epsom.
2013 Dubai Sheema Classic, Nad Al Sheba.

Jonjo O'Neill

Jackdaws Castle, Cotswolds

Born in County Cork in 1952, Jonjo left school to join Michael Connolly as an apprentice. In his mid-twenties, he broke the record belonging to his close friend, Ron Barry, by riding the most winners in one season in 1977/78. He was best known for riding Sea Pigeon and the ill-fated mare, Dawn Run, the only horse to win a Champion Hurdle and a Gold Cup. Jonjo began training in 1986, the same year he was diagnosed with cancer, which he thankfully overcame. He remains the only person to have ridden and trained 100 winners in a season. Jonjo is based at Jackdaws Castle in the Cotswolds, and trains many horses owned by legendary punter J. P. McManus. His greatest wins have come when providing Tony McCoy with his elusive Grand National win with Don't Push It, and when Synchronised won the Gold Cup. Jonjo has trained three winners at the Cheltenham Festival five times in the last twelve years, and has handled the likes of Exotic Dancer, dual Cheltenham winner Albertas Run and the ill-fated Synchronised, who was homebred by J.P. McManus.

Notable Past Winners

Albertas Run
2008 RSA Chase, Cheltenham, 2010 Melling Chase, Aintree & 2011 Ryanair Chase, Cheltenham.

Don't Push It
2010 Grand National, Aintree.

Holywell
2014 Mildmay Novices' Chase, Aintree.

More Of That
2014 World Hurdle, Cheltenham.

Shutthefrontdoor
2014 Irish Grand National, Fairyhouse.

Synchronised
2012 Gold Cup, Cheltenham.

Taquin De Seuil
2012 Challow Hurdle, Newbury &
2014 JLT Novices' Chase, Cheltenham.

Tominator
2013 Northumberland Plate, Newcastle.

David Pipe

Nicholashayne, Somerset

David Pipe is the son of 15-time Champion trainer Martin Pipe, the most successful National Hunt trainer of all time. David spent years assisting his father before taking out the licence, but also sought experience with Michael Dickinson in the US and Cricquette Head-Maarek in France. He also trained point-to-pointers for six years, training 164 winners in this time. He was the first trainer to train a hundred winners in his first season and has enjoyed consistent success every year since, in quality and quantity. David trained a Grand National winner in his second season, with Comply Or Die, and has been successful at the highest level with Madison Du Berlais, Lough Derg, Dynaste and Our Vic. David enjoys an even flow of decent horses from France and Ireland, virtually guaranteed to produce a stable star every season.

Most Notable Winners

Comply Or Die
2008 Grand National, Aintree.

Dynaste
2012 Feltham Novices' Chase, Kempton.
2014 Ryanair Chase, Cheltenham.

Grands Crus
2011 Feltham Novices' Chase, Kempton.

Madison Du Berlais
2008 Hennessy Gold Cup, Newbury.

Moon Racer
2015 Champion Bumper, Cheltenham.
2015 Weatherbys Champion Bumper, Cheltenham.

Our Vic
2008 Ryanair Chase, Cheltenham.
2008 Totesport Bowl, Aintree.

The Liquidator
2013 Champion INH Bumper, Punchestown.

Un Temps Pour Tout
2015 Grande Course de Haies D'Auteuil, Auteuil.

Western Warhorse
2014 Arkle Chase, Cheltenham.

Sir Michael Stoute

Freemason Lodge, Newmarket

Sir Michael was born in Barbados, where he lived to the age of nineteen, before coming to Britain in the 1960s to assist Malton trainer Pat Rohan. Rohan had already been a mentor to former 'cock of the North' jockey Edward Hide, as well as the likes of Richard Fahey and Jimmy Quinn. Sir Michael took out his own licence in 1972, and has since been crowned champion trainer ten times. He famously trained the ill-fated Shergar to win the Epsom Derby by a staggering ten lengths in 1981. Two years later, the horse was kidnapped and held to ransom, never to be seen again. The thieves have never been identified, though the most popular theory holds the IRA responsible for the bungled plot. Sir Michael is the only trainer in the 20th century to win a British Classic for five successive seasons. He received a knighthood in 1998, curiously for services to tourism in Barbados, and more recently trained the Queen's horse, Estimate, to win the Ascot Gold Cup at the Royal meeting. Sir Michael has been responsible for some magnificent horses, such as King's Theatre, Pilsudski, Ezzoud, Singspiel, Daliapour, Islington, Russian Rhythm, Conduit and Kris Kin, as well as those mentioned here.

Most Notable Recent Winners

Ask
2009 Coronation Cup, Epsom.

Dank
2013 Beverley D Stakes, Arlington & 2013 Breeders' Cup Fillies' and Mares' Turf, Santa Anita.

Estimate
2013 Gold Cup, Royal Ascot.

Harbinger
2010 King George VI and Queen Elizabeth Diamond Stakes, Ascot.

Hillstar
2015 Canadian International Stakes, Woodbine.

Integral
2015 Sun Chariot Stakes, Newmarket.

Workforce
2010 Derby, Epsom & 2010 Prix de l'Arc de Triomphe, Longchamp.

Roger Varian

Kremlin House Stables, Newmarket

After a brief career as a conditional jockey, Roger joined Newmarket trainer Michael Jarvis as an assistant, after a riding accident in the US cut short his career as a jockey. During his ten years spent with Jarvis, he was involved in the training of five-time Group 1 winner, Rakti, as well as Oaks winner Eswarah and the speedy Iffraaj. Upon Jarvis' retirement in 2011, due to illness, Roger took over the reins at Kremlin House, named by a Russian prince who built the yard in the late nineteenth century. Roger's first runner was fourth at the Dubai Carnival, whilst his first British runner, Eton Forever, won the Spring Mile at Doncaster. He trained a Group 1 winner in his first season, and has continued that trend every year since. Kingston Hill became his first Classic winner when taking the St Leger in 2014, helping to contribute to the yard's £3 million prize money world-wide that season. He also handled the 2014 Champion two-year-old, Belardo.

Most Notable Recent Winners

Ambivalent
2013 Pretty Polly Stakes, The Curragh.

Belardo
2014 Dewhurst Stakes, Newmarket.

Cursory Glance
2014 Moyglare Stud Stakes, The Curragh.

Farraj
2013 John Smith's Cup, York.

Kingston Hill
2013 Racing Post Trophy, Doncaster.
2014 St Leger, Doncaster.

Vert de Grace
2014 Criterium de St Cloud, St Cloud.

www.gentingclubriverlights.co.uk
RESTAURANT ENTERTAINMENT
AXOM

The Everam System

Each of the following pages 44 to 47 lists selected racecourses with specific race distances and high or low draw.

The selection is based on aspects of the draw but only in HANDICAP RACES with a minimum of 10 horses declared to run. It is also influenced by a particular jockey riding in that race.

The actual selection is narrowed down to the FIVE highest or lowest drawn horses (see pages 44 to 47). Then to determine the actual selection, take the highest rated jockey from the list below, within the selected drawn numbers.

JOCKEY RATINGS	
Ryan Moore	10
William Buick	9
James Doyle	8
Frankie Dettori	7
Silvestre de Sousa	6
Paul Hanagan	5
Graham Lee	4
George Baker	3
Andrea Atzeni	2
Danny Tudhope	1

BATH

LOW NUMBERS
up to 1m

BEVERLEY

LOW NUMBERS (unless soft)
up to 1m

BRIGHTON

LOW NUMBERS
up to 7f

CARLISLE

LOW NUMBERS
over 5f and 6f

CATTERICK

LOW NUMBERS
up to 7f

CHEPSTOW

HIGH NUMBERS
up to 1m

CHESTER

LOW NUMBERS

EPSOM

HIGH NUMBERS
5f

GOODWOOD

LOW NUMBERS
up to 7f

HAMILTON

HIGH NUMBERS
5f, 6f

HAYDOCK

HIGH NUMBERS
5f, 6f

LINGFIELD (turf)

HIGH NUMBERS
up to 7f

MUSSELBURGH

HIGH NUMBERS
up to 7f

NOTTINGHAM

HIGH NUMBERS
5f, 6f

REDCAR

MID TO HIGH NUMBERS
up to 1m

SALISBURY

LOW NUMBERS
up to 7f

WARWICK

LOW NUMBERS
5f

YARMOUTH

HIGH NUMBERS
5f, 6f

How to Locate the Winner of The Grand National

The Grand National is an epic race run over the marathon distance of just under four and a half miles at Aintree, near Liverpool. The race has been run most years since 1839, when runners in that inaugural race had to negotiate a stone wall, situated where the water jump is now, two hurdles and a large brook. The latter obstacle has since been named after Captain Becher, who scrambled for salvation after falling during the maiden running. The race soon took shape as we recognise it today, with thirty differing obstacles, to prove a unique challenge for horse and rider. The only time the race has been run away from Aintree was during the War, when it was run at the now long-gone Gatwick racecourse.

After complaints from protestors, the course has been modified recently to make racing safer for the horses. Brooks and drops on the landing side of fences have been levelled out, and the fourth fence, which proved the most difficult to jump statistically (after Becher's Brook), has been lowered. Each jump has a plastic base with rubber padding, and is covered in over a foot in height of freshly cut spruce. The start was also brought 90 yards closer to the first fence, to reduce speed on approach and give the horses a fairer start. Statistics can point us in the right direction when searching for a selection, and can indeed rule many of the forty-runner field out. These are outlined below.

- **The mighty five-time Festival winner Golden Miller is the only horse to have ever won the Cheltenham Gold Cup and the Grand National in the same season, back in 1934. The most recent to try was the ill-fated Synchronised, back in 2012.**

- There have only ever been three grey winners of the Grand National, the last being Neptune Collonges in 2012.

- **There have been very few winning mares in the race, the last being Nickel Coin in 1951.**

- You have to go back to 1940 to find a winner of the race younger than 8.

- **You have to go even further to 1923 to find a winning horse older than 12.**

- It is essential to have winning form over 3 miles or further. The last winner not to have won over as far as 3 miles was Gay Trip back in 1970.

- **Interestingly, 6 of the last 10 winners have run over hurdles during the current season prior to their Grand National victory, presumably to protect their handicap mark.**

To conclude, our selection tends to be a gelding, aged between 9 and 12, with a weight between 10st 4lbs and 11st 6lbs. The horse must have run in at least 10 steeplechases and won over 3 miles.

How To Locate the Winner of The Derby

The Epsom Derby is a national institution. The race was devised at a drinks party after the first running of the Oaks, where Lord Derby and Lord Bunbury were said to have flipped a coin to decide who the race would be named after. The race began in 1780 on Epsom Downs over a distance of one mile. Four years later, the race was lengthened to a mile and a half, and included the infamous Tattenham Corner, which turns into the home straight. The very tight bend features an adverse camber, and caused many horses to slip and fall in years gone by. Famously, the suffragette Emily Davison was killed by King George V's horse, Anmer, as it rounded Tattenham Corner in the 1913 Derby. As an activist, she had intended to cause a distraction by running onto the course, with the King watching, rather than to commit suicide.

The race is obviously much safer nowadays, but is still a most extreme test of a horse, meaning the best horse does not always necessarily win, due to the nature of the course. Even the great Dancing Brave could not cope with Epsom in 1986, finishing second to Shahrastani; his only defeat. There are, once again, a series of statistics that can help us find the winner:

- **Only one winner in the past ten years has been priced above 7/1.**
- Favourites have a good record in the race, recent winners being Camelot and Australia.
- **There has been just one French-trained winner in the past 30 years, Andre Fabre's Pour Moi.**
- The last grey horse to win the Derby was Airborne in 1946.
- **Ruler Of The World was the first horse to win wearing cheekpieces, in 2013.**
- All of the last 10 winners of the race had raced within 35 days of the race, and had not been unplaced that season.

- **In the past 10 Derbys, 9 winners had begun their careers over 7 furlongs or more, with only Sir Percy beginning his career over 6 furlongs.**

- In the past 10 years, half of the winners had won or been placed in the Guineas. The Dante Stakes at York provides the next best guide, with two winners and a second-placed horse progressing to win the Derby.

Derby day at Epsom Racecourse

Tipster Scams

You will have discovered all about the bookmakers 'overround' elsewhere in this book. Without this 'profit margin' there would be no such thing as bookmaking. Coupled with the fact that there are so many events that can influence the outcome of any horse race, you should beware of any tipster telling you that he or she has the magic formula to beat the bookies.

Furthermore, if anyone did acquire the magic formula of how to consistently make a profit from betting on horses, then the last thing that person would do, would be to tell another soul how it's done, or which horses this formula is indicating will win particular races.

Fortunately, most punters are well aware of the reality of betting on horses. However, there are gullible people who are easily tricked into paying money to a stranger, for racing tips or systems that will produce a stream of future winners and massive profits beyond their wildest dreams.

The fraudsters who perpetrate these betting scams leave a trail of disappointment, heartbreak and severe financial loss to people who can often ill afford to be scammed in such a manner.

In July 2013, one of the biggest betting fraud cases of all time was heard at Lewes Crown Court, where three alleged fraudsters were accused of scamming £5million from vulnerable people.

The jury had to sit through weeks of evidence, which included one heartbreaking story after another.

The ploys used to trick victims into parting with their cash included a multitude of scams. However, all of the scams appeared to be the same ones that have dogged the racing industry for decades and still plague us all today.

The following paragraphs will enlighten you and hopefully help you to never fall for any scam offer that may drop through your letterbox or be transmitted via the internet.

Scam 1

Lewes Crown Court was told that the defendants posted numerous unsolicited brochures to lists of people believed to be interested in betting. In turn, punters sent cheques in payment for betting information. However, in return, the defendants didn't supply anything at all and when people complained, their complaints were ignored.

Scam note 1: *This is a common scam for countless products and services, not just betting information. The moral is to never send any payment to anyone unless you are convinced that they are genuine. The problem with printed brochures and internet websites is that sophisticated technology is available for just about anyone to produce an offer that will look highly professional. So do beware, the brochure may look genuine, but may not be. Scam 1 is perhaps the easiest to perpetrate. Cheque payments are easy for the scammers to hide through a multitude of accounts (including foreign banks).*

Scam 2

The court was told that one of the defendants played on his notoriety of being banned from racecourses for his involvement in alleged fraudulent betting activity. The defendant used this fact to make it appear to gullible consumers that he was paying insiders for betting information that the authorities treated as a type of 'insider knowledge' that created an unfair advantage over bookmakers and other punters.

Scam note 2. *This is a common ploy and is sadly going on day after day. Sometimes the fraudsters even pretend to be banned. The gullible victims appear to overlook the fact that the offer is being made by someone who is openly admitting they are breaking the rules of racing and acting in a manner that could be illegal. Effectively, consumers are being invited to take advantage of fraudulent activity. Do you really want to send your hard-earned cash to such individuals? Sadly, the court was told of numerous cases where huge sums of money were handed over.*

Scam 3

The court was told that the defendants made it appear that they were so successful at making a profit from betting, their betting accounts were shut down by bookmakers. Some brochures included images of cheques that appeared to be from high street bookmakers, for huge sums of money.

Scam note 3. *Even if a cheque is genuine, it does not necessarily prove that it was in payment for a huge win on the horses (or whatever).*

Scam 4

The court was told that once a consumer handed money over, other offers would be made to them. This included an offer to get involved in the importation of racehorses for up to £10,000 a time, which would then be sold on for massive profits.

Scam note 4. *Again, this appears to be a case of the offer being portrayed in a glossy, genuine-looking brochure, or by means of a clever talking sales person on the telephone. Once a scammer has your telephone number, the vulnerability level increases dramatically.*

Scam 5

The court was told that a punter had paid a defendant the sum of £49 to subscribe to a particular service and, after backing a winner from the first tip, was then invited to join a 'Special Betting Service' for £5,000. The victim paid the defendant in full, by cheque.

Scam note 5. *If a fraudster strikes lucky and selects a winner with the first tip, the punter is lulled into a very dangerous false security. The belief is that all the claims made in the glossy brochure are really true. Hence in this actual case at Lewes Crown Court, the victim told the jury that this was what happened to him.*

Scam 6

The court was told that a punter was invited to bet £20,000 on a particular horse at 4-1, on behalf of a defendant. The deal was that if the horse won, the punter would pay £40,000 of the £80,000 winnings to the defendant and if it didn't win, the defendant would repay the punter his full £20,000. The ploy was that the defendant was barred from placing such a large bet himself because he was so successful at winning and bookmakers refused to take his bets. In the event, the victim was unable to raise £20,000 and only staked £3,600. The horse lost and the victim was never reimbursed.

Scam note 6. *This is one of the oldest tricks in the book. Remember it and never fall for it.*

When summing up the case for the jurors, the judge at Lewes Crown Court told them; "some of you may consider the victims in this case are gullible people, foolish and maybe even greedy. They had forgotten the old saying that if something looks too good to be true, it generally is".

The jury went away to consider the evidence presented to them and returned with GUILTY verdicts for all three defendants. The judge handed out two sentences of four years each and one of five years.

In a statement, a spokesperson for Sussex Police said; "this case serves as a timely reminder to punters, be very careful about trusting your money to anyone".

Betting Slang

Much of the language is rhyming slang or tic tac. For example, 6/4, which is 'ear 'ole', is tic tac, raise hand to ear to represent those odds.

ODDS	SLANG	ODDS	SLANG
Evens	Levels	**9/2**	On the shoulders
11/10	Tips	**5/1**	Hand
6/5	Sais a ching	**11/2**	Hand and a half
5/4	Wrist	**6/1**	Exes
11/8	Up the arm	**13/2**	Exes and a half
6/4	Ear 'ole	**7/1**	Neves
13/8	Bits on the ear 'ole	**15/2**	Neves and a half
7/4	Shoulder	**8/1**	T. H.
15/8	Double taps	**9/1**	Enin
2/1	Bottle	**10/1**	Net
9/4	Top of the head	**11/1**	Elef
5/2	Face	**12/1**	Net and bice
11/4	Elef a vier	**14/1**	Net and rouf
3/1	Carpet	**16/1**	Net and ex
100/30	Burlington Bertie	**20/1**	Score
7/2	Carpet and a half	**25/1**	Pony
4/1	Rouf	**33/1**	Double carpet

CHELTENHAM

BRITISH CHAMPION FLAT JOCKEYS

Year	Jockey	Wins	Year	Jockey	Wins
2014	**Richard Hughes**	161	1980	**Willie Carson**	166
2013	**Richard Hughes**	208	1979	**Joe Mercer**	164
2012	**Richard Hughes**	172	1978	**Willie Carson**	182
2011	**Paul Hanagan**	165	1977	**Pat Eddery**	176
2010	**Paul Hanagan**	191	1976	**Pat Eddery**	162
2009	**Ryan Moore**	174	1975	**Pat Eddery**	164
2008	**Ryan Moore**	186	1974	**Pat Eddery**	148
2007	**Seb Sanders/Jamie Spencer**	190	1973	**Willie Carson**	164
2006	**Ryan Moore**	180	1972	**Willie Carson**	132
2005	**Jamie Spencer**	163	1971	**Lester Piggott**	162
2004	**Frankie Dettori**	192	1970	**Lester Piggott**	162
2003	**Kieren Fallon**	207	1969	**Lester Piggott**	163
2002	**Kieren Fallon**	136	1968	**Lester Piggott**	139
2001	**Kieren Fallon**	166	1967	**Lester Piggott**	117
2000	**Kevin Darley**	155	1966	**Lester Piggott**	191
1999	**Kieren Fallon**	200	1965	**Lester Piggott**	160
1998	**Kieren Fallon**	204	1964	**Lester Piggott**	140
1997	**Kieren Fallon**	202	1963	**Scobie Breasley**	176
1996	**Pat Eddery**	186	1962	**Scobie Breasley**	179
1995	**Frankie Dettori**	211	1961	**Scobie Breasley**	171
1994	**Frankie Dettori**	233	1960	**Lester Piggott**	170
1993	**Pat Eddery**	169	1959	**Doug Smith**	157
1992	**Michael Roberts**	206	1958	**Doug Smith**	165
1991	**Pat Eddery**	165	1957	**Scobie Breasley**	173
1990	**Pat Eddery**	209	1956	**Doug Smith**	155
1989	**Pat Eddery**	171	1955	**Doug Smith**	168
1988	**Pat Eddery**	183	1954	**Doug Smith**	129
1987	**Steve Cauthen**	197	1953	**Sir Gordon Richards**	191
1986	**Pat Eddery**	176	1952	**Gordon Richards**	231
1985	**Steve Cauthen**	195	1951	**Gordon Richards**	227
1984	**Steve Cauthen**	130	1950	**Gordon Richards**	201
1983	**Willie Carson**	159	1949	**Gordon Richards**	261
1982	**Lester Piggott**	188	1948	**Gordon Richards**	224
1981	**Lester Piggott**	179	1947	**Gordon Richards**	269

3

Apprentice Jockeys

An apprentice is an inexperienced jockey that rides on the Flat. He or she is employed by a licensed trainer, and is able to ride in races from the age of sixteen. When an apprentice begins his or her career, they will claim a seven-pound weight allowance to counterbalance their inexperience against their more experienced colleagues that have 'ridden out' their allowance. Once the apprentice has ridden the winners of 20 races, their claim will be reduced to five pounds until they ride fifty winners (forty for conditionals), when they will only claim three pounds. The apprentice will have no claim when they have ridden 95 winners. They must then compete on a level playing field with other professionals.

Once the jockey has reached the age of twenty-five, they will lose their claim regardless of how many winners they have ridden, although conditional riders are allowed another year's grace. The last apprentice to win a Classic was Jamie Spencer, aged 17, when he won the Irish 1,000 Guineas on Tarascon. Britain's first female apprentice champion was Hayley Turner, who shared the title with Saleem Golam in 2005. In National Hunt races, apprentice jockeys are known as 'conditional' riders, and also have a claim. Theirs is lost sooner, after just 75 winners, though conditionals can claim an additional three pounds allowance until they have ridden three winners and when riding for their employer.

BRITISH CHAMPION APPRENTICE JOCKEYS

Year	Jockey	Wins	Year	Jockey	Wins
2014	**Oisin Murphy**	74	2003	**Ryan Moore**	59
2013	**Jason Hart**	51	2002	**Paul Hanagan**	83
2012	**Amy Ryan**	40	2001	**Chris Catlin**	72
2011	**Martin Harley**	57	2000	**Lee Newman**	63
2010	**Martin Lane**	41	1999	**Robert Winston**	49
2009	**Frederik Tylicki**	60	1998	**Carl Lowther**	72
2008	**William Buick & David Probert**	50	1997	**Royston Ffrench**	77
2007	**Greg Fairley**	65	1996	**Dane O'Neill**	79
2006	**Stephen Donohoe**	44	1995	**Seb Sanders**	61
2005	**Hayley Turner & Saleem Golam**	44	1994	**Steven Davies**	45
2004	**Tom Queally**	59	1993	**David Harrison**	40

BRITISH CHAMPION NATIONAL HUNT JOCKEYS

Season	Jockey	Wins	Season	Jockey	Wins
2014-15	**Tony McCoy**	231	1980-81	**John Francome**	105
2013-14	**Tony McCoy**	218	1979-80	**Jonjo O'Neill**	115
2012-13	**Tony McCoy**	185	1978-79	**John Francome**	95
2011-12	**Tony McCoy**	199	1977-78	**Jonjo O'Neill**	149
2010-11	**Tony McCoy**	218	1976-77	**Tommy Stack**	97
2009-10	**Tony McCoy**	195	1975-76	**John Francome**	96
2008-09	**Tony McCoy**	186	1974-75	**Tommy Stack**	82
2007-08	**Tony McCoy**	140	1973-74	**Ron Barry**	94
2006-07	**Tony McCoy**	184	1972-73	**Ron Barry**	125
2005-06	**Tony McCoy**	178	1971-72	**Bob Davies**	89
2004-05	**Tony McCoy**	200	1970-71	**Graham Thorner**	74
2003-04	**Tony McCoy**	209	1969-70	**Bob Davies**	91
2002-03	**Tony McCoy**	258	1968-69	**Terry Biddlecombe/Bob Davies**	77
2001-02	**Tony McCoy**	289	1967-68	**Josh Gifford**	82
2000-01	**Tony McCoy**	191	1966-67	**Josh Gifford**	122
1999-00	**Tony McCoy**	245	1965-66	**Terry Biddlecombe**	102
1998-99	**Tony McCoy**	186	1964-65	**Terry Biddlecombe**	114
1997-98	**Tony McCoy**	253	1963-64	**Josh Gifford**	94
1996-97	**Tony McCoy**	190	1962-63	**Josh Gifford**	70
1995-96	**Tony McCoy**	175	1961-62	**Stan Mellor**	80
1994-95	**Richard Dunwoody**	160	1960-61	**Stan Mellor**	118
1993-94	**Richard Dunwoody**	197	1959-60	**Stan Mellor**	68
1992-93	**Richard Dunwoody**	173	1958-59	**Tim Brookshaw**	83
1991-92	**Peter Scudamore**	175	1957-58	**Fred Winter**	82
1990-91	**Peter Scudamore**	141	1956-57	**Fred Winter**	80
1989-90	**Peter Scudamore**	170	1955-56	**Fred Winter**	74
1988-89	**Peter Scudamore**	221	1954-55	**Tim Molony**	67
1987-88	**Peter Scudamore**	132	1953-54	**Dick Francis**	76
1986-87	**Peter Scudamore**	123	1952-53	**Fred Winter**	121
1985-86	**Peter Scudamore**	91	1951-52	**Tim Molony**	99
1984-85	**John Francome**	101	1950-51	**Tim Molony**	83
1983-84	**John Francome**	131	1949-50	**Tim Molony**	95
1982-83	**John Francome**	106	1948-49	**Tim Molony**	60
1981-82	**John Francome/Peter Scudamore**	120	1947-48	**Bryan Marshall**	66

CITIPOST

FRANCISCLARK
MILDREN

Permutations

A permutation (perm) is a fixed combination of selections of results. If, for example, a pools company invites you to select ten home teams to win from a list of 49 matches, you can either just select one line of ten selections, which is not a permutation or, if you want to increase your chances of winning, you can introduce one or more extra selections, but to save you writing out dozens or hundreds of lines of ten selections, all the possibilities are covered in a permutation. For example, if you want to perm twelve teams to win at home, your instructions to the pools firm would be to mark twelve selections in one line and write on the coupon 'perm any ten from twelve'.

To find the number of lines your selections cover, take the actual number of selections and multiply backwards for the number of fixed selections. In this example any ten from twelve selections would be 12x11x10x9x8x7x6x5x4x3 (that's twelve selections), so start with the figure twelve and multiply backwards consecutively for the ten units of the fixed combination. The answer being 239,500,800; this is then divided by the number of the fixed combinations multiplied consecutively 1x2x3x4x5x6x7x8x9x10. This gives 3,628,800 and with the help of your trusty calculator you will quickly find the answer being 66. Therefore at 10p a line your twelve selections cover 66 x 10p, a total cost of £6.60.

The same formula can be used to find doubles, trebles, etc., from your racing selections. If you select six horses in six different races and want to cover all the possibilities of trebles coming up within those selections, you are in fact doing a permutation of any three from six. Take the number of selections (6) and multiply backwards for the number of fixed combinations (3)=6x5x4 divided by 1x2x3=20 trebles.

There are excellent multiple bet calculators on the internet now, which makes it much easier when calculating the odds and possibilities of each bet.

No. of selections	Double	Treble	4 fold	5 fold	6 fold	7 fold	8 fold	9 fold	10 fold
2	1								
3	3	1							
4	6	4	1						
5	10	10	5	1					
6	15	20	15	6	1				
7	21	35	35	21	7	1			
8	28	56	70	56	28	8	1		
9	36	84	126	126	84	36	9	1	
10	45	120	210	252	210	120	45	10	1

Betting Options

Betting Shops opened for the first time in Britain in 1961. Prior to their creation, betting was only permitted on-course or via a credit account, although gambling occurred illegally on street corners and in other non-licensed areas. Betting shops were commonly perceived as dank, dark rooms and were not generally attractive to enter. Attending betting shops was largely frowned upon by society, not helped by the deliberately shady cosmetic appearance of the venues. Thankfully, this is not the case nowadays, as shops are now bright, lively places and are plentiful in most towns. In the early years following their opening, races were not allowed to be screened live, nor were drinks permitted to be sold to shop customers.

Betting Shops

The Betting and Gaming Act 1960 legalised betting shops in the United Kingdom, and the first shop opened in May 1961. Nowadays there are approximately 150 betting shops per million people in the population. The highest concentration is in the West Midlands and West Yorkshire regions, whereas Cornwall has one of the lowest. The three biggest bookmaking chains are Ladbrokes, William Hill and Coral. Collectively they are known as "The Big Three". A licensed bookmaker can legally offer bets on the outcome of any event (except for the National Lottery).

Betting Accounts

Most bookmakers offer deposit accounts. Money can be stored with the bookmaker using a debit or credit card, and bets can be placed until this amount has gone. The advantage of having an account is you can bet from anywhere as long as you possess either a phone or a computer. Each punter is issued with a user ID and an account number for ease of use and to maintain security. Online gambling is now a massive industry, especially after the creation of Betfair, which will be covered later.

Betting Tax and Commissions

The world of betting celebrated an historic day on October 6th, 2001, when off-course betting tax was abolished. This detracted from the value of going racing, when the massive 9% tax was waived. Betting exchanges don't charge tax, but are different in that they charge 'commission' on winning bets, with the rate of commission varying according to the aggregate amount you stake.

Betting Exchanges

Betting exchanges are a relatively new betting phenomenon that have revolutionised the way punters can stake their money on just about any event possible. They are often seen to provide better value than traditional bookmakers, as there is no 'over round', which puts the odds in the bookmaker's favour. Betting exchanges enable punter to punter betting, with the consumer devising their own odds for each selection. As long as these odds are considered reasonable by another punter who wishes to 'lay' the bet, the bet will be matched and is therefore in place.

The betting exchange concept began in 2000 when Flutter.com began what they described as 'open market betting'. Eventually the company merged with Betfair and Sporting Options to become the most potent exchange on the planet. The betting exchange concept suits both large and small-stake punters, as you only pay commission on winnings, starting at 5%. The commission percentage lowers as turnover increases on the account.

An advantage with betting exchanges is that there is occasionally the opportunity to 'hedge your bets', and create a betting opportunity where you can't lose. For instance, if you back a horse at 8/1 (displayed on screen as 9.00), and he is backed into 4/1 (5.00), you can then LAY at the smaller price to cover the value of your stake. You can also bet 'in running', i.e. mid-race or during a football match, for instance. After a bet is placed, a time delay is used to allow punters to cancel unmatched bets that have no chance of returning a profit. It is worth remembering that pictures shown on the television are delayed a few seconds from the live event, so punters at the racecourse are always at an advantage.

Disadvantages are that there are no credit facilities available, even for regular punters. Loyalty to regular punters is shown by a lowering of the commission rate. There are also fewer options for multiple bets for the punter who enjoys a Lucky 15, for instance. Betfair remains the market leader by some distance, and is a major sponsor of sporting events.

Spread Betting

Spread betting is the concept of wagering on an event where the payoff directly relates to the accuracy of the outcome. A spread bet is not as simple as winning and losing and is a volatile form of punting, where high losses are possible, so much so that spread betting firms are regulated by the Financial Conduct Authority rather than the Gambling Commission.

Spread betting provides a large quantity of different opportunities on a wide range of sporting events.

E.g. with horseracing, you can bet on the 'Winning Distances'. If the bookmaker thinks the cumulative total of the individual horses' winning distances throughout the day at Brighton will be 28 - 30 lengths, and you feel there will be some close finishes, you would choose to 'sell' at 28. Your stake is £2 per point. If the total winning distance is 15 lengths, you would win (28 - 15) = 13 x 2 = £26 winnings. Conversely, if you are mistaken and the distances are massive, and total 50 lengths, the outcome would be (50 - 30) = 20 x 2 = lose £40. This is when the nature of spread betting is most volatile, as there is no particular limit set on a subject like this, so the losses can be great.

There is also the option of 'cashing out' at any stage, where the punter can either choose to secure a profit, rather than risking going the full term of the bet, or can limit a loss if the result clearly isn't going in your favour.

For certain sports, e.g. football, Sporting Index offer a more fixed index on certain outcomes, for instance, the Champions' League Outright Index, where the winner is awarded 100 pts, the runner up 75 pts, so you know when placing the bet the best and worst case scenario, which relates to potential profit or loss.

As well as many possible sporting events, or irregular events such as X Factor or the General Election, many people choose to bet on city indexes. Some gamblers prefer to spread bet rather than buy and sell shares, as there is no income tax to pay on winnings and no commission either.

Each Way Betting

This is the betting that is generally offered by most bookmakers.

RUNNERS	FRACTION	PLACINGS	TYPES OF RACE
1-5	-	Win only	All
6-7	1/4 the odds	2nd only	All
8-11	1/5 the odds	2nd & 3rd	Only in handicaps
8+	1/5 the odds	2nd & 3rd	All
12 - 15	1/4 the odds	2nd & 3rd	Only in handicaps
16 +	1/4 the odds	2nd, 3rd & 4th	Only in handicaps

Example: *A selection finishes third at 5/1 in a nine-horse race. A £10 each way bet (costing a total of £20) would return a total of £20, as the win part of the bet is lost and the place odds equate to an even money winning bet.*

Double

A total of two selections are made in separate events. The total return, plus the stake, are then automatically placed on the second part of the bet. Both selections must win, or be placed for an each-way double.

Treble

The same principles as the Double, but with a third selection.

Example: *Three selections all win at odds of 2/1, 4/1 and 6/1, with £1 staked to win.*
£1 x 2/1 = Collect £3, including £1 stake.
£3 x 4/1 = Collect £15, including £3 stake.
£15 x 6/1 = Collect £90, including £15 stake.
Total return is £105

Accumulator

Four selections are chosen, all must win or be placed (for betting each-way) for the bet to continue to accumulate.

Trixie

Three selections are chosen for four bets, including one treble and three doubles.

Patent

The same basis as the Trixie, but with three single bets as well, totalling seven bets.

Yankee

Four selections, totalling eleven bets. This bet is a permutation of six doubles, four trebles and one fourfold accumulator.

Lucky 15

The same as the Yankee, but this also includes four single bets, totalling fifteen.

Super Yankee

Sometimes known as the 'Canadian' or ‘Alphabet’. There are five selections with this bet including one fivefold accumulator, five fourfold accumulators, ten trebles and ten doubles, totalling twenty-six bets.

Lucky 31

Same as Super Yankee, but with five single bets also, totalling 31 bets.

Heinz

Named due to its 57 bet makeup. Six selections are chosen to create one sixfold accumulator, six fivefold accumulators, fifteen fourfolds, twenty trebles and fifteen doubles.

Lucky 63

Same as Heinz, but also includes 6 singles, totalling 63 bets.

Super Heinz

The Super Heinz is a 7 selection wager consisting of 120 bets: 21 doubles, 35 trebles, 35 four-folds, 21 five-folds, 7 six-folds and a seven-fold accumulator.

Goliath

A massive bet, as the name would suggest. This is a total of 247 bets, including 28 doubles, 57 trebles, 70 four folds, 56 five folds, 28 six folds, 8 seven folds and one eight fold. Eight winners would yield a massive winning amount!

Tricast

The first three home in a race must be selected in the correct order. The dividend is calculated by computer and is not based on the starting prices of the runners. Although only single bets are accepted, permutations are possible. To perm three selections, six bets would be required, to perm four selections twenty-four are required, to perm five selections sixty are required, to perm six then one hundred and twenty are required and a perm of seven selections would be two hundred and ten bets. These bets are only available on selected races.

Example Race
Five horses selected:
Yeats, Honolulu, Distinction, Mad Rush, Regal Flush.

The bookmaker is instructed to place a Full Cover Permutation Tricast = sixty bets at £1 units = £60 staked.

Computer Straight Forecast (CSF)

The first and second past the post must be selected in the correct order. Unlike Tote pools, the dividend that is returned is not based on the total amount placed on the race you are interested in, but is calculated by computer using a complicated formula after the race.

When there is an odds-on favourite that you think will win, it can often be an idea to try to back the horse with another in a forecast, or Exacta. You can occasionally find good value forecasts, especially if you fancy a horse to finish second at a decent price. Bookmakers can publish prices for straight-forecasts, and they can provide some value.

READY RECKONER

S.P.	50p	£1	£2	£3	£5	£10	£20
1/3	0.67	1.33	2.67	4.00	6.67	13.33	26.67
2/5	0.70	1.40	2.80	4.20	7.00	14.00	28.00
4/9	0.72	1.44	2.89	4.33	7.22	14.44	28.89
1/2	0.75	1.50	3.00	4.50	7.50	15.00	30.00
4/7	0.79	1.57	3.14	4.71	7.86	15.71	31.43
8/13	0.81	1.62	3.23	4.85	8.08	16.15	32.31
4/6	0.83	1.67	3.33	5.00	8.33	16.67	33.33
8/11	0.86	1.73	3.45	5.18	8.64	17.27	34.55
4/5	0.90	1.80	3.60	5.40	9.00	18.00	36.00
5/6	0.92	1.83	3.67	5.50	9.17	18.33	36.67
10/11	0.95	1.91	3.82	5.73	9.55	19.09	38.18
Evens	1.00	2.00	4.00	6.00	10.00	20.00	40.00
11/10	1.05	2.10	4.20	6.30	10.50	21.00	42.00
6/5	1.10	2.20	4.40	6.60	11.00	22.00	44.00
5/4	1.13	2.25	4.50	6.75	11.25	22.50	45.00
11/8	1.19	2.38	4.75	7.13	11.88	23.75	47.50
6/4	1.25	2.50	5.00	7.50	12.50	25.00	50.00
13/8	1.31	2.63	5.25	7.88	13.13	26.25	52.50
7/4	1.38	2.75	5.50	8.25	13.75	27.50	55.00
15/8	1.44	2.88	5.75	8.63	14.38	28.75	57.50
2/1	1.50	3.00	6.00	9.00	15.00	30.00	60.00
9/4	1.63	3.25	6.50	9.75	16.25	32.50	65.00
5/2	1.75	3.50	7.00	10.50	17.50	35.00	70.00
11/4	1.88	3.75	7.50	11.25	18.75	37.50	75.00
3/1	2.00	4.00	8.00	12.00	20.00	40.00	80.00
10/3	2.17	4.33	8.67	13.00	21.67	43.33	86.67
7/2	2.25	4.50	9.00	13.50	22.50	45.00	90.00
4/1	2.50	5.00	10.00	15.00	25.00	50.00	100.00
9/2	2.75	5.50	11.00	16.50	27.50	55.00	110.00
5/1	3.00	6.00	12.00	18.00	30.00	60.00	120.00
11/2	3.25	6.50	13.00	19.50	32.50	65.00	130.00
6/1	3.50	7.00	14.00	21.00	35.00	70.00	140.00
13/2	3.75	7.50	15.00	22.50	37.50	75.00	150.00
7/1	4.00	8.00	16.00	24.00	40.00	80.00	160.00
15/2	4.25	8.50	17.00	25.50	42.50	85.00	170.00
8/1	4.50	9.00	18.00	27.00	45.00	90.00	180.00
17/2	4.75	9.50	19.00	28.50	47.50	95.00	190.00
9/1	5.00	10.00	20.00	30.00	50.00	100.00	200.00
10/1	5.50	11.00	22.00	33.00	55.00	110.00	220.00
11/1	6.00	12.00	24.00	36.00	60.00	120.00	240.00
12/1	6.50	13.00	26.00	39.00	65.00	130.00	260.00
14/1	7.50	15.00	30.00	45.00	75.00	150.00	300.00
16/1	8.50	17.00	34.00	51.00	85.00	170.00	340.00
20/1	10.50	21.00	42.00	63.00	105.00	210.00	420.00
25/1	13.00	26.00	52.00	78.00	130.00	260.00	520.00
33/1	17.00	34.00	68.00	102.00	170.00	340.00	680.00

Charity Race Nights

This is quite big business for the firms that compile and supply the films (of horse races) for showing at charity events. They can also be useful profit-making ventures for good causes.

However, there's no excuse for punters to be treated shabbily by offering unfair odds. A well run charity will respect the fact that the punters are there to be entertained and many of them love the thrill of backing winners and getting some prize money back.

It would not be unreasonable for a charity to run a tote for the evening and to take up to 50% of the money bet on each race and then divide the remainder amongst those punters who managed to select the winner.

However, there appears to be a growing trend for holiday companies to run these race nights as part of the evening entertainment. A few are thought to possibly be creaming off around 50% of the total staked, which, given that it's not for charity and the punters have already paid for their nightly entertainment as part of the holiday ticket price, may be viewed by some as rather unacceptable.

Three tests were performed at three different venues and each one paid out sums that were suspiciously low.

All of the tests involved races with eight runners and no clues given to the punters before the races of the actual ability or form of the horses taking part in each race. The punters were betting blindly, win only, £2 per ticket, on a series of eight numbers (1 to 8).

These race nights should never be taken seriously and stakes (at commercial venues) should possibly be limited to small fun bets only. However, where the race evening is being run for charity, perhaps, then, caution can be thrown to the wind.

BHA & Inside Information

The British Horseracing Authority (BHA) is the regulatory body in the sport of horse racing. One department that has been much enhanced in recent times is the Integrity, Legal and Risk Department, who aim to achieve "a combined strategy of fairness, education, prevention and deterrence."

The BHA seeks to identify and deter any breach of regulations within the sport. They also investigate any malpractice or beach of the rules, gather information regarding potential wrong-doing and monitor real-time betting markets for suspicious betting activity. The BHA works closely with betting exchange firms and is informed when unusual betting patterns emerge. The BHA also inspects the yards of licensed trainers to check everything is above board, and that they have the correct facilities at their disposal, as well as policing the weighing room and stables on a raceday. For instance, jockeys are not permitted to use a mobile phone in an unsupervised area whilst at the races, or they face a £250 fine.

The integrity of racing has come under more scrutiny since betting exchanges have become such a popular method of gambling. They give unscrupulous owners and connections the chance to 'lay' their own horses when they thought they could not win, therefore profiting from the horse losing. The problem comes when action is taken by connections to prevent the horse from succeeding, by giving the jockey poor instructions, or by racing the horse whilst he is unfit, for instance, so he cannot perform at his best.

Inside Information is regarded as information into the likely participation and performance of a horse in a race, which is known by the trainer, owner, rider, stable employees and even service providers (e.g. the vet or farrier), which is not in the public domain. There is a point of contact within the BHA called 'Race Straight', where anyone can raise alarm if they feel there has been a breach. In 2013, there were 3,500 instances of suspected foul-play, resulting in just 75 investigations, including failed horse and rider drugs tests, financial irregularities and equine welfare. This is a very small number, considering how many races that take place every year.

The BHA is naturally very keen to keep British horseracing a very clean sport. The entry point for an offence relating to integrity and inside information is three years, with the possibility of being 'warned off' for five years. To be 'warned off' means that you cannot set foot on licensed property, which includes racecourses, training yards and public training grounds, such as Newmarket. British horseracing is among the cleanest in the world, thanks to the vigilance of the BHA. Recently, well established racing professionals such as Eddie Ahern, Dean McKeown and Karl Burke have all paid their price for what may have been a foolish indiscretion that has lead to period of disqualification.

WHITE ROSE
SADDLERY

14

BRIGH

Lycetts
3

1

11

18
mayiclaim
Stobart

2

MARTYN
Roy Christie
CORAL

Fund

British Racecourses

	Flat Turf	National Hunt	Flat All Weather
Aintree		✓	
Ascot	✓	✓	
Ayr	✓	✓	
Bangor		✓	
Bath	✓		
Beverley	✓		
Brighton	✓		
Carlisle	✓	✓	
Cartmel		✓	
Catterick	✓	✓	
Chelmsford City			✓
Cheltenham		✓	
Chepstow	✓	✓	
Chester	✓		
Doncaster	✓	✓	
Epsom	✓		
Exeter		✓	
Fakenham		✓	
Ffos Las	✓	✓	
Fontwell		✓	
Goodwood	✓		
Hamilton	✓		
Haydock	✓	✓	
Hexham		✓	
Huntingdon		✓	
Kelso		✓	
Kempton		✓	✓
Leicester	✓	✓	
Lingfield	✓	✓	✓
Ludlow		✓	
Market Rasen		✓	
Musselburgh	✓	✓	
Newbury	✓	✓	
Newcastle		✓	✓
Newmarket	✓		
Newton Abbot		✓	
Nottingham	✓		
Perth		✓	
Plumpton		✓	
Pontefract	✓		
Redcar	✓		
Ripon	✓		
Salisbury	✓		
Sandown	✓	✓	
Sedgefield		✓	
Southwell		✓	✓
Stratford		✓	
Taunton		✓	
Thirsk	✓		
Towcester		✓	
Uttoxeter		✓	
Warwick*	✓	✓	
Wetherby	✓	✓	
Wincanton		✓	
Windsor	✓		
Wolverhampton			✓
Worcester		✓	
Yarmouth	✓		
York	✓		

* Warwick was not staging Flat racing at time of publication.

Flat Racecourses

Ascot

A stiff, right-handed galloping track with a straight mile. A low draw has a slight advantage when stalls are on the stands' side on the straight course.

○ **Jockey:** Ryan Moore ○ **Trainer:** Richard Hannon

Ayr

A fast, left-handed track with minor undulations, long straights and sweeping bends. Low numbers favoured.

○ **Jockey:** Graham Lee ○ **Trainer:** Jim Goldie

Bath

A left-handed course with a slight chicane down the back straight. The run-in is on the turn throughout, as are the five and six furlongs chutes. Those drawn low in sprints are favoured unless the ground is soft.

○ **Jockey:** Luke Morris ○ **Trainer:** Richard Hannon

Beverley

A very stiff right-handed track, galloping in nature. The seven-furlong course is especially severe and a real test for juveniles. It is ideal to be drawn low in races of less than a mile (unless soft).

○ **Jockey:** Silvestre de Sousa ○ **Trainer:** Mark Johnston

Brighton

A horse-shoe shaped track that is very undulating and has a variety of cambers. There is a need to be fast away in sprints, and a low draw is a definite advantage on good ground. Does not suit the long-striding galloper.

○ **Jockey:** Silvestre de Sousa ○ **Trainer:** Richard Hannon

Carlisle

A very stiff, right-handed track with the last half mile sharply against the collar. Ground can prove very testing after excess rainfall. Low draws are usually best in races over 5f and 6f.

○ **Jockey:** Graham Lee ○ **Trainer:** Kieth Dalgleish

Catterick

A very sharp left-handed track that is always on the turn. The course is undulating and suits horses that race prominently. Low numbers are best round here up to seven furlongs.

○ **Jockey:** Silvestre de Sousa ○ **Trainer:** Richard Fahey

Chelmsford City

A new development that ressurrected the former Great Leighs course, built on the old Essex Showground. The all-weather circuit is a popular, left-handed galloping oval run on Polytrack. There is limited data at this stage to support a draw bias.

○ **Jockey:** Jamie Spencer ○ **Trainer:** William Haggas

Chepstow

A long left-handed course that has severe undulations throughout. The course has a straight mile, which is largely downhill. When the stalls are on the stands side in sprints it is an advantage to be drawn high against the rail, especially in soft ground. Ground can become extremely testing at times.

○ **Jockey:** David Probert ○ **Trainer:** Bernard Llewellyn

Chester

A flat, left-handed course that is virtually spherical. A low draw is essential, as is a good start, as it is very difficult to make up ground if you get trapped wide on the course.

○ **Jockey:** Francis Norton ○ **Trainer:** Richard Fahey

Doncaster

A left-handed galloping track with long, sweeping bends. It is a very fair course with both round and straight miles. A high draw is best in sprint races.

○ **Jockey:** Jamie Spencer ○ **Trainer:** Richard Fahey

Epsom

A famous horseshoe shaped left-handed course with severe undulations and cambers. The course is only a mile and a half in length, with a steep rise during the first quarter mile and then a severe drop into the straight around the tight Tattenham Corner, which has a severe camber to provide a real test. The five-furlong track is the fastest in the world, as it is downhill for the first half mile. You want a high draw in sprints, and a low draw from seven to ten furlongs.

○ **Jockey:** David Probert ○ **Trainer:** Richard Hannon

Ffos Las

A flat, left-handed galloping oval course that is a mile and a half round.
○ **Jockey:** Martin Dwyer ○ **Trainer:** Bernard Llewellyn

Goodwood

An unconventional figure of eight track with many turns and severe undulations and cambers. The finish is sited on a separate chute. The course suits the versatile type that is well balanced. The sprint course rises sharply for a furlong and is then downhill to the finish. Low numbers have an advantage in sprints and high draws on the round course are also preferred.
○ **Jockey:** William Buick ○ **Trainer:** Richard Hannon

Hamilton

A very stiff course with a loop at the end of the straight, so for longer races runners must start past the winning post and go down the track before turning the loop and coming towards home, where the finish is uphill. Mid to high draws are generally favoured in sprints, especially in soft ground.
○ **Jockey:** Joe Fanning ○ **Trainer:** Mark Johnston

Haydock

A flat, left-handed galloping track, which is very fair. High draws are preferable in soft ground sprints.
○ **Jockey:** Richard Kingscote ○ **Trainer:** Mark Johnston

Kempton

A deluxe all-weather track has now replaced the Flat turf course. There are two separate courses for different distances and both are fair. This course can attract the higher quality all-weather horse and has a good reputation with trainers. Horses drawn low seem to have an advantage in races up to a mile. The only right-handed all-weather track in the country.
○ **Jockey:** Jim Crowley ○ **Trainer:** Richard Hannon

Leicester

A stiff, right-handed track that often provides quite testing ground after rainfall. Horses must stay well here and handle the slight undulations. High numbers are best in sprints, especially when the ground is soft.
○ **Jockey:** Paul Hanagan ○ **Trainer:** Richard Hannon

Lingfield

The turf course is left-handed with a steep climb in the back straight, which falls away entering the home straight. The course is stiff with a five and a half furlong straight, favouring those drawn high. The all-weather course is tighter and is inside the turf track, with less steep gradients. High numbers are still at an advantage in turf sprints.
○ **Jockey:** Jim Crowley ○ **Trainer:** Richard Hannon

Musselburgh

A right-handed track with long straights and sharp bends. The track is virtually flat throughout. Favours the handy type with plenty of speed, and high draws are helpful up to a mile.
○ **Jockey:** Joe Fanning ○ **Trainer:** Richard Fahey

Newbury

A flat, left-handed course that is very galloping in nature and is a fair test. There are straight and round mile courses with a high draw bias up to a mile, especially in soft ground.
○ **Jockey:** Silvestre de Sousa ○ **Trainer:** Richard Hannon

Newcastle

At the time of printing a new all-weather course run on Tapeta is currently being built.

Newmarket

There are two racecourses, the Rowley Mile, which is used in the spring and autumn, and the July Course, which is used during the summer months. The Rowley Mile's course is wide and two and a quarter miles in length, with a ten-furlong run-in. The famous dip, two furlongs from home, catches out inexperienced horses and those with doubtful stamina. The July Course is similar, with a slight climb inside the final furlong. Draw bias depends on where the stalls are sited, as the course is so wide.
○ **Jockey:** Ryan Moore ○ **Trainer:** Richard Hannon

Nottingham

A left-handed, galloping course with sweeping bends. High numbers are preferred on the straight course, as are low numbers on the round course.
○ **Jockey:** Silvestre de Sousa ○ **Trainer:** Richard Hannon

Pontefract

A very stiff left-handed track that is two miles round. The home turn is uphill, then falls away into the straight, which is about a quarter of a mile in length. Stamina is essential. Low numbers are favoured in sprints.

○ **Jockeys:** Silvestre de Sousa ○ **Trainer:** Richard Fahey

Redcar

A long, flat left-handed course with tight bends. There is a straight mile track, where there is a mid to high draw bias.

○ **Jockey:** Danny Tudhope ○ **Trainer:** Richard Fahey

Ripon

A sharp, right-handed oval track that is mainly flat. It is an advantage to race up with the pace at this venue. Low draws are helpful on the sprint course, except when the ground is soft.

○ **Jockey:** P J McDonald ○ **Trainer:** Tim Easterby

Salisbury

A straight course with a tight loop at the top of the track, which allows races up to a mile and six furlongs. The course is stiff, with a steady climb to the line, so stamina is essential. High numbers are favoured on the straight course when the ground is good. Low numbers are preferred in sprints when the ground is soft as runners may cross to the stands rail.

○ **Jockey:** James Doyle ○ **Trainer:** Richard Hannon

Sandown

A stiff, right-handed galloping track that suits horses drawn high. There is a separate five-furlong course, which dissects the round course and is on the collar throughout.

○ **Jockey:** Ryan Moore ○ **Trainer:** Richard Hannon

Southwell

A tight left-handed all-weather circuit with low draws a preference over six furlongs. The course is flat and the surface is considerably slower and deeper than any other all-weather course.

○ **Jockey:** Joe Fanning ○ **Trainer:** Michael Appleby

Thirsk

A flat, left-handed oval track with sharp bends and a run-in of about half a mile. Low numbers are favoured on the round course and high numbers on the straight course.

○ **Jockey:** Danny Tudhope ○ **Trainer:** Tim Easterby

Warwick

(Warwick are not currently running Flat races after an incident on the track. They plan to open the course again in the near future.) A sharp, left-handed track with separate five-furlong chute, which contains a sharp bend. Low numbers are a great advantage, especially over five furlongs.

○ **Jockey:** Tom Queally ○ **Trainer:** Richard Hannon

Wetherby

A mainly flat, left-handed course that has trialled Flat racing in 2015, with a view to being granted more fixtures. The meetings were well supported by top trainers, who were very complimentary about the course. There is not enough data at present to form a reliable draw bias.

○ **Jockey:** Paul Mulrennan ○ **Trainer:** Eric Alston

Windsor

A figure-of-eight course that now only holds Flat racing after the National Hunt course closed. High numbers are favoured in sprints, as the stands rail is a very important factor. It is more difficult for horses to win in the centre of the track unless the ground is soft.

○ **Jockey:** Ryan Moore ○ **Trainer:** Richard Hannon

Wolverhampton

A left-handed, all-weather track, run on Tapeta, a newly-installed surface. It is too soon to report whether a draw bias has appeared.

○ **Jockey:** Luke Morris ○ **Trainer:** Mark Johnston

Yarmouth

A long, flat, left-handed galloping track with sharp bends. The ground is usually good or faster with racing being well supported by Newmarket trainers. The course has a straight mile, slightly favouring high numbers.

○ **Jockey:** Ryan Moore ○ **Trainer:** William Haggas

York

A flat, left-handed course that is two miles in length. The course is very wide and fair, and holds top-class racing, suiting long-striding gallopers. When the ground is soft, low to middle draws can be favoured over shorter distances.
○ **Jockey:** Ryan Moore ○ **Trainer:** Richard Fahey

National Hunt Racecourses

Aintree

A fast, flat left-handed track with regulation fences on the Mildmay course that catch many out due to the speed they are going. Results can often differ from Cheltenham at the National Meeting, as there are no major undulations, suiting the speedier type of horse. The Grand National course is two and a quarter miles in length with sixteen unique fences. The jumps have been made safer in recent years, but the course itself remains the ultimate test for horse and rider in Britain.
○ **Jockey:** Richard Johnson ○ **Trainer:** Nicky Henderson

Ascot

A right-handed galloping track with stiff fences and an uphill finish. The run-in is not very long and many races are decided around the final turn. Suits the thorough stayer and accurate jumper.
○ **Jockey:** Richard Johnson ○ **Trainer:** Nicky Henderson

Ayr

A fair and flat left-handed track with well presented fences. The ground can become testing through the winter. Suits front-runners.
○ **Jockey:** Peter Buchanan ○ **Trainer:** Lucinda Russell

Bangor

An undulating left-handed track in North Wales and is the only licensed track not to have a grandstand. Favours the handy type as the course is always on the turn. The fences are not the most demanding.
○ **Jockey:** Richard Johnson ○ **Trainer:** Donald McCain

Carlisle

A very stiff right-handed track that can become stamina sapping after persistent

rain. There is a long pull up to the line, so horses have to stay very well indeed, and the fences can catch out tired horses.
○ **Jockey:** Brian Hughes ○ **Trainer:** Donald McCain

Cartmel

This holiday course only has a handful of meetings, but attracts bumper crowds and decent fields. The quality of racing can be moderate. A tight, turning left-handed track that throws some unusual results, and boasts the longest run-in of half a mile after the last obstacle.
○ **Jockey:** Brian Hughes ○ **Trainer:** Donald McCain

Catterick

A very tight, left-handed undulating course that attracts low grade horses. This track only suits very nippy horses, as they are always on the turn. The ground can be testing in the winter and the fences are uncomplicated.
○ **Jockey:** Brian Hughes ○ **Trainer:** Donald McCain

Cheltenham

Renowned as the home of National Hunt racing, and quite deservedly so. The racing is top quality, the fences are notoriously tricky and stiff, and are the ultimate test for any horse, away from Aintree's National fences. Stamina is essential as there is a stiff climb to the finish, where results often change. There are several different courses at Cheltenham, though all are undulating, left-handed and testing.
○ **Jockey:** Barry Gerraghty ○ **Trainer:** Paul Nicholls

Chepstow

An undulating left-handed track with long straights. The ground can become very testing in mid-winter and suits the robust and thorough stayer. The fences are straightforward, though can catch out tired horses running home on the five-furlong home straight.
○ **Jockey:** Richard Johnson ○ **Trainer:** Philip Hobbs

Doncaster

A stiff, left-handed track with sweeping bends and is flat in the main, except for Rose Hill at the end of the back straight. The course drains very well, and has become very popular with trainers after long periods of wet weather as the ground is seldom as heavy as it is elsewhere.
○ **Jockey:** James Reveley ○ **Trainer:** Nicky Henderson

Exeter

A very stiff, galloping course that is very undulating and about two miles around. The fences are all uphill, so the venue is popular for novice chasers. Runners have to jump the last four fences uphill so can get very tired.

○ **Jockey:** Nick Scholfield ○ **Trainer:** Philip Hobbs

Fakenham

A square left-handed track of about a mile round with uncomplicated fences. Runners are always on the turn, so suits the handy type with doubtful stamina. The course is flat and attracts low quality horses. The ground stays quite good throughout the year.

○ **Jockey:** Leighton Aspell ○ **Trainer:** Nicky Henderson

Ffos Las

A flat, left-handed course that is big and galloping, and is very well supported by Welsh and Irish trainers.

○ **Jockey:** Paul Moloney ○ **Trainer:** Evan Williams

Fontwell

The only figure-of-eight National Hunt course in Britain is the Fontwell chase course, which not all horses handle. Results can change approaching the line over both obstacles, so avoid betting in running. The hurdles track is left-handed and conventional with four flights to a one-mile circuit, and a slight rise to the line. Both tracks are tight and suit prominent runners.

○ **Jockey:** Tom Cannon ○ **Trainer:** Chris Gordon

Haydock

A left-handed galloping track, suiting the long-striding individual. Racing is generally of a decent quality.

○ **Jockey:** Jason Maguire ○ **Trainer:** Donald McCain

Hexham

A particularly undulating left-handed course with a very long run-in. The fences are fair, though the track can require plenty of stamina in winter conditions. Horses run downhill through the back straight and then sharply uphill to the line.

○ **Jockey:** Brian Hughes ○ **Trainer:** Lucinda Russell

Huntingdon

A completely flat, right-handed oval track that suits front-runners.
○ **Jockey:** Aidan Coleman ○ **Trainer:** Nicky Henderson

Kelso

A left-handed, undulating track where a mixture of speed and stamina is required. The going is reasonable throughout the winter, but the turns are tight and the run-in is a testing two furlongs. The hurdles track is two furlongs shorter in circumference than the chase track.
○ **Jockey:** Brian Hughes ○ **Trainer:** Donald McCain

Kempton

A completely flat, right-handed track with decent fences and quality racing. This track does not necessarily suit the non-stayer, as this galloping track puts an emphasis on speed and accurate jumping.
○ **Jockey:** Barry Geraghty ○ **Trainer:** Nicky Henderson

Leicester

A demanding right-handed track with sharp bends, long straights and slight undulations. The fences are decent and favours good jumpers, especially in novice chases. The ground can often become quite heavy, putting emphasis on stamina.
○ **Jockey:** Sam Twiston Davies ○ **Trainer:** Nigel Twiston Davies

Lingfield

The course is left-handed, undulating and suited to handy types that stay well.
○ **Jockey:** Paddy Brennan ○ **Trainer:** Jonjo O'Neill

Ludlow

A completely flat, right-handed track where runners continually cross public roads covered up with large mats. The fences are not the most substantial though claim casualties, as runners continually go a fast gallop. Usually drier than most other tracks through the winter.
○ **Jockey:** Paul Moloney ○ **Trainer:** Evan Williams

Market Rasen
Slightly undulating right-handed track with easy fences. Suits front-runners as the course is fairly easy in nature. Holds the most valuable summer jumping race fixture as well as meetings all year round.
○ **Jockey:** Richard Johnson ○ **Trainer:** Charlie Longsdon

Musselburgh
A very tight, right-handed track with stiffish fences located in the long straights. The bends are tight, and the course is level throughout, suiting front-runners.
○ **Jockey:** Peter Buchanan ○ **Trainer:** Lucinda Russell

Newbury
This left-handed track attracts top-class fields with plenty of prize-money available. The course itself is basically flat, with sweeping bends and long straights. The fences are big and stiff, but are well presented. Stamina is essential, as the ground can become very testing in wet weather.
○ **Jockey:** Richard Johnson ○ **Trainer:** Nicky Henderson

Newcastle
A gruellingly stiff, left-handed track, where the ground is often soft. The fences are testing and racing is competitive.
○ **Jockey:** James Reveley ○ **Trainer:** Lucinda Russell

Newton Abbot
A left-handed track that suits speedy horses. They only tend to race in the dryer months as the course does not drain well. The fences are uncomplicated, but require a quick jumper or too much ground is lost. Front-runners have an advantage here.
○ **Jockey:** Richard Johnson ○ **Trainer:** Paul Nicholls

Perth
A very popular track that is the most northern in the UK. The track resembles a horizontally-dissected triangle, and is sharp, left-handed and flat with uncomplicated fences. The ground can be very testing, though the racing is always well supported by southern and Irish trainers, making the racing competitive and very popular with owner, trainers and racegoers alike.
○ **Jockey:** Jason Maguire ○ **Trainer:** Gordon Elliott (Ire)

Plumpton

A tight, left-handed track with a stiff uphill rise from the home turn and then a long downhill run in the back straight. The ground is often very testing in the winter, but they seldom lose a meeting through waterlogging.

○ **Jockey:** Tom Scudamore ○ **Trainer:** Gary Moore

Sandown

Another scenic right-handed track with big, stiff park fences that cause a variety of complications. The famous Railway Fences are the last three fences in the back straight and are taken in rapid succession. The finish is uphill and the result often changes after the last, so don't bet in running.

○ **Jockey:** Barry Geraghty ○ **Trainer:** Paul Nicholls

Sedgefield

An undulating, left-handed track that accommodates low quality horses. Runners must stay well here when the ground is soft, but can be lucky when the ground is firm if short of stamina.

○ **Jockey:** Brian Hughes ○ **Trainer:** Donald McCain

Southwell

A very tight, left-handed track with challenging portable fences that seem to claim plenty of victims. The ground can be very testing and front-runners are suited here, as are accurate jumpers.

○ **Jockey:** Richard Johnson ○ **Trainer:** Jonjo O'Neill

Stratford

Another flat, left-handed track that races often during the summer. They are generally able to provide safe going and are well supported therefore, with big fields. The fences are straightforward and accommodating, especially to front-runners.

○ **Jockey:** Richard Johnson ○ **Trainer:** Tim Vaughan

Taunton

An almost flat right-handed track with sharp bends, suiting the handy type. The fences are not complicated, though are often taken at speed and require accuracy. Front-runners favoured.

○ **Jockey:** Nick Scholfield ○ **Trainer:** Paul Nicholls

Towcester
Probably the stiffest (right-handed) track around, as the final half mile is uphill. The fences are average, but are taken both up and downhill and can cause problems. Stamina is quite essential as the last two fences in particular are on a steep incline, which can affect the result.
○ **Jockey:** Paddy Brennan ○ **Trainer:** Kim Bailey

Uttoxeter
Mainly flat, left-handed track with sharp bends and a chicane in the back straight. The ground can be very testing, especially for the Midlands National meeting, which is run the day after the Cheltenham Festival.
○ **Jockey:** Richard Johnson ○ **Trainer:** Donald McCain

Warwick
Mainly flat left-handed track with just one rise to the ditch in the back straight before the ground sweeps away from you, leading you to a line of five fences. The obstacles are especially uncomplicated and the ground can be very soft in the winter.
○ **Jockey:** Sam Twiston Davies ○ **Trainer:** Alan King

Wetherby
Mainly flat, left-handed track with big, stiff fences that command plenty of respect. Suits long-striding gallopers and accurate jumpers.
○ **Jockey:** Brian Hughes ○ **Trainer:** Sue Smith

Wincanton
This right-handed track can provide superb ground throughout the winter along with top quality racing. The course dries very quickly and requires a speedy horse, as the course is mainly flat.
○ **Jockey:** Daryl Jacob ○ **Trainer:** Paul Nicholls

Worcester
Racing only takes place at Worcester through the summer, as the course is badly affected by flooding through the winter. The fences are easy, in two long straights, but the hurdles are the 'fixed brush' variety and don't suit every horse.
○ **Jockey:** Tom Scudamore ○ **Trainer:** Paul Nicholls`

Point-to-Pointing

Point-to-point racing is amateur steeplechasing organised by local hunts or clubs. It is more regionalised than National Hunt racing, with each area boasting a group of very enthusiastic participants. The racing season begins at the end of November, and continues until the middle of June, with meetings generally run at weekends. They are not usually run at recognised racecourses, but on temporary locations, usually farm land within the territory of the organising hunt or club. The races are run over steeplechase fences. The meetings are very well organised and can be very popular, especially when the weather is good to bring out the crowds.

The majority of races are run over three miles, with some maiden races run over two and a half miles. Races differ in class according to how many races you have won. Horses start in maiden races, then progress to Restricted races (restricted to horses that have only won a maiden or hunt members' race). The next step is Intermediate races, which are also open horses that have won a National Hunt Flat race. The highest level races are 'Opens', which are open to all, though a horse usually carries a weight penalty after winning two open races. 'Confined' races are also popular, which are confined to horses qualified with neighbouring hunts, i.e. for horses trained within the locality. The BHA rating of a horse is totally irrelevant, which makes the sport very attractive to older horses that have begun to struggle in N.H. races. Weights are level in all races, unless horses carry a penalty for certain wins, or have allowances for age and/or their sex. It is common to see well-known handicap chasers providing experience for young jockeys across the country. Recent examples include Ghizao, Join Together and Prospect Wells.

The sport is also a useful opportunity for young horses to gain experience rather than competing in N.H. Flat races. Many trainers, like Paul Nicholls especially, draft out some of their more backward horses to gain racing experience, before they have them back to train themselves. These horses boast greater racing experience than their peers, and often better jumping technique, having already raced over fences. This also counts for young jockeys, many of whom gain experience in the sport before furthering their careers. Excellent riders like Tom O'Brien, Nick Scholfield and Daryl Jacob all began by riding plenty of point-to-point winners, before becoming successful professional jockeys.

The best 'pointers' progress to run in Hunter Chases, the feature races being the Foxhunters' at Cheltenham, Punchestown and Aintree (over the Grand National fences), and the Stratford Champion Foxhunters' Chase. In the past the sport has been considered a largely amateur or 'hobby' sport for many, but with the money trainers like Tom Lacey and Paul Nicholls are putting into the sport, the standards are continually rising, with some seriously good young horses and well-known handicappers bringing in the crowds. Most courses boast excellent facilities, with bookmakers, food and drink marquees and closer access to the horses and riders.

Points of the Racehorse

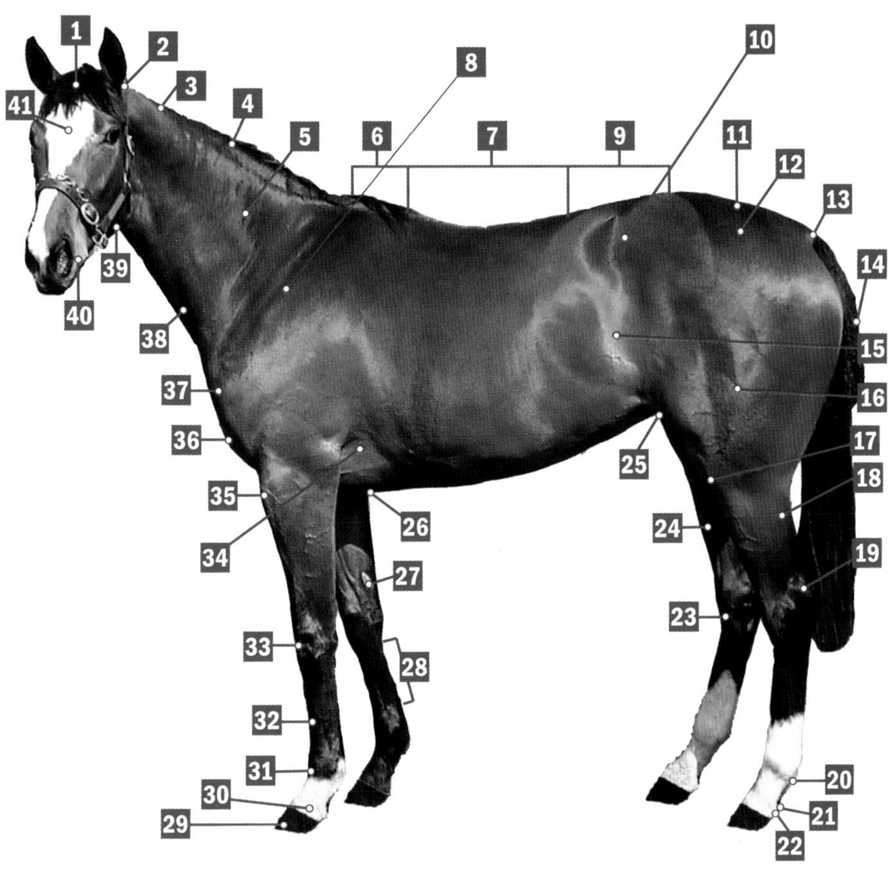

1	Forelock	**12**	Quarters	**23**	Hock joint	**34**	Brisket
2	Poll	**13**	Dock	**24**	Gaskin	**35**	Forearm
3	Crest	**14**	Tail	**25**	Sheath	**36**	Breast
4	Mane	**15**	Flank	**26**	Point of elbow	**37**	Point of shoulder
5	Neck	**16**	Thigh	**27**	Chestnut	**38**	Windpipe
6	Withers	**17**	Stifle joint	**28**	Back tendons	**39**	Throat
7	Back	**18**	Hamstring	**29**	Wall of hoof	**40**	Muzzle
8	Shoulder	**19**	Point of hock	**30**	Coronet	**41**	Forehead
9	Loins	**20**	Ergot	**31**	Fetlock		
10	Point of hip	**21**	Pastern	**32**	Cannon		
11	Croup	**22**	Heel	**33**	Knee		

Action of the Racehorse

High Knee Action

Racehorses with a high knee action are usually suited to soft or heavy ground and is more commonly seen in Jumpers. As well as the 'rounded' action being better suited to soft ground, horses with this type of knee action tend to hit the ground with more force and so soft ground will decrease the risk of injury.

Low Knee Action

Racehorses with a low knee action are usually better suited to fast ground. They use less energy to create their stride pattern and soft ground would blunt their speed and compromise their 'quick' action.

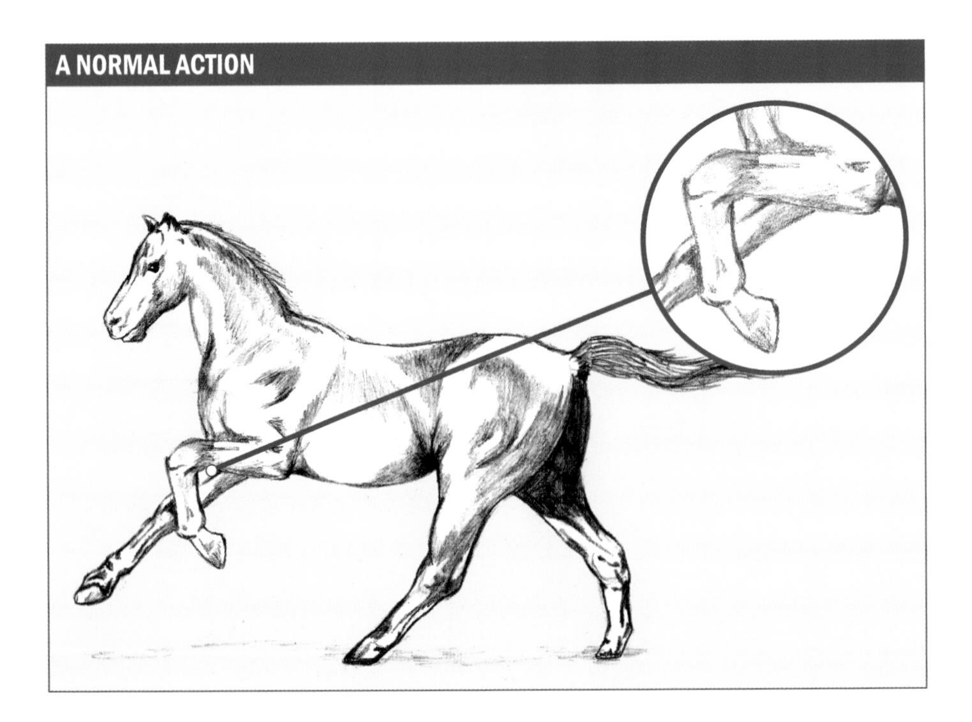
A NORMAL ACTION

A HIGH ACTION

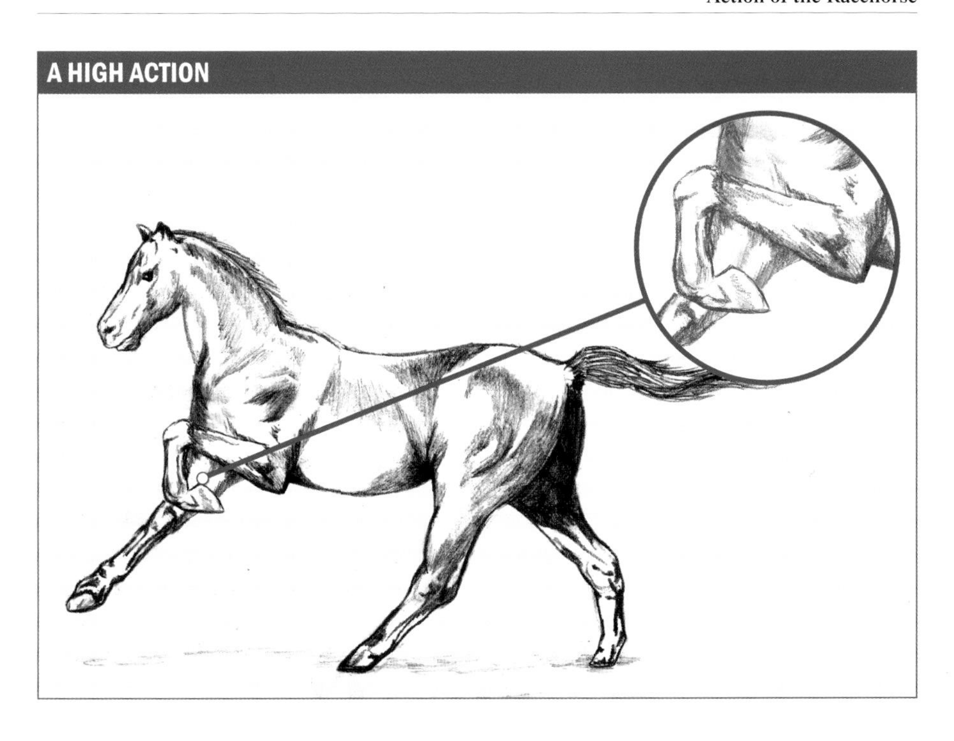

A LOW ACTION

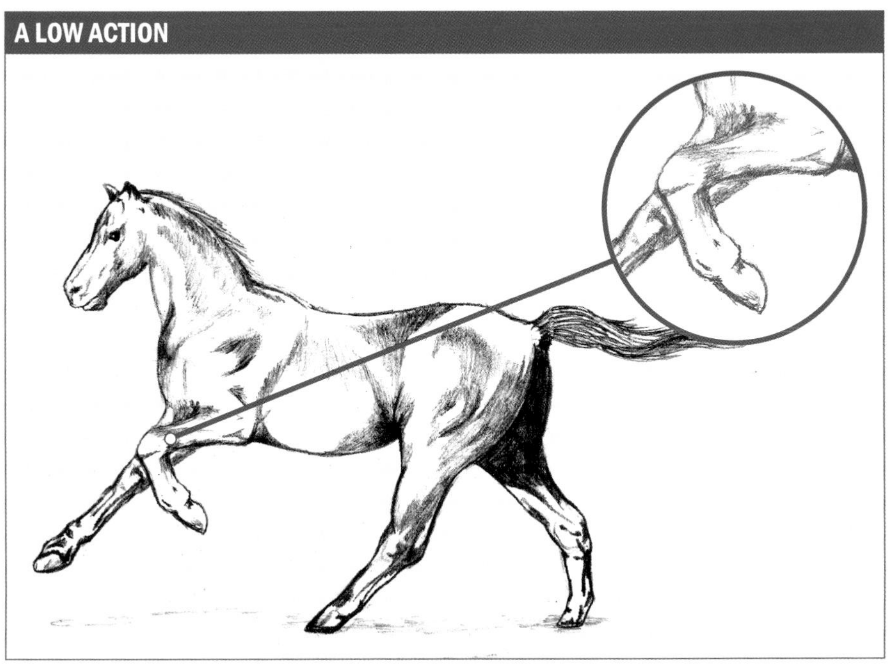

Racing Clubs

The difference between a racing club and a racing syndicate is that normally the members of a club are buying into the entertainment of following the horses owned by the club, they don't actually own the horses.

Elite Racing Club is the leading racing club in Great Britain and as well as having a string of racehorses in training, there's a very successful breeding programme that has produced some high-profile winners, including Soviet Song, Ribbons, Penzance and Dandino.

Details of how to join Elite Racing Club can be found on the website:
www.eliteracingclub.co.uk

Or by telephoning:
01380 811699

Or by writing to Elite Racing Club, P.O. Box 100, Devizes, SN10 4TE

Soviet Song and Johnny Murtagh

Racing Syndicates

If you are thinking about joining a racing syndicate, do tread carefully. Some syndicates pretend to offer shared racehorse ownership, but in reality they are racing clubs.

Axom is one of the leaders and offers real racehorse ownership shares.

Axom's Irving, Paul Nicholls' 100th Grade 1 winner, under Nick Scholfield

Details of how to buy a share in a racehorse with Axom, can be found at the website: www.axom.co.uk or by writing to Axom, P.O. Box 100, Devizes, SN10 4TE or phone 01380 811777.

Owners Group

'Owners Group' is a racehorse syndicate business that splits ownership shares into very small units, thereby giving everyone the opportunity to own a share in a racehorse.

The cost of one share can be as low as £34 and that price includes all the associated costs to keep, train and race the horse for a specified period of time.

'Owners Group' is a subsidiary business of the long established Elite Racing Club and Axom.

Like other racing syndicates, this is not an investment opportunity and nobody should buy a share if they are hoping to make a profit. It is all about the fun and enjoyment of getting involved in racehorse ownership.

Details of how to become a part owner in a racehorse can be found on the website; www.ownersgroup.co.uk or can be obtained by writing to Owners Group, P.O. Box 100, Devizes, SN10 4TE or phone 01380 811888.

Big Divi

This is one of Britain's most popular large syndicates.

Subscribers pay £2 to have the newsletter posted to them every week. The price includes postage & packing and is great value for money. They also pay £3 towards the weekly syndicate pot.

The syndicate spends by far the largest chunk of the weekly fund (approximately 70%) on a Tote Scoop6 entry for Saturday racing and also plays the Lotto, Thunderball and EuroMillions. The smallest percentage of the syndicate pot is spent on various racing and football bets, including the pools.

Whilst the aim is to scoop as many big jackpot wins as possible, the emphasis is firmly on fun and entertainment. Any winnings that the syndicate receives is equally divided between the subscribers.

Full details can be found on the website: www.bigdivi.co.uk or by writing to Big Divi, P.O.Box 100, Devizes, SN10 4TE or phone 01380 811700.

Horseracing Memorabilia

With over 200 years of history, the sport of horseracing has a phenomenal amount of memorabilia for collectors to collect and traders to trade.

Some specialist auction houses have sold amazing items related to the world of horseracing, including the original gates from Ascot Racecourse.

Amongst the most popular items at affordable prices are racecourse badges, racecards, books, autographs, postcards, games, magazines, cigarette cards, trophies and much more.

▲ **The Handicap Race Game.** (1950). Tinplate. 220mm diameter. Spinning arrow stops on the winning horse. In full working order. Unknown maker. Game (g). Original box (f) £18 - £22

▲ **Jockey model.** Plastic. John Smith (race sponsor). (1990). (ex) £3 - £5

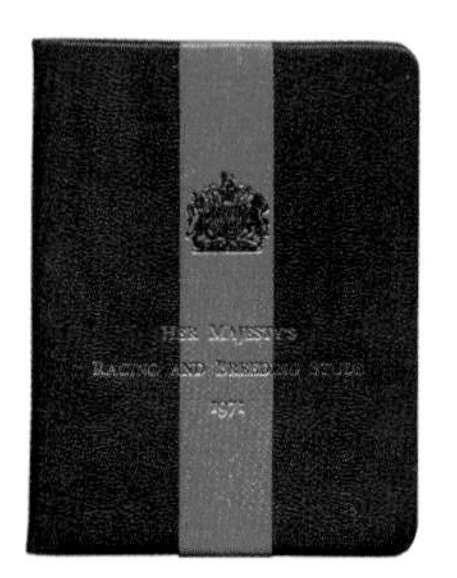

▲ **Her Majesty's Racing & Breeding Studs.** 1971. Imitation leather cover. 100 pages. 150 x 120mm (vg). £6 - £8

▲ **Racing Annual 1951.** News of the World paperback book. 164 pages. Includes some superb advertisements from pools companies, bookmakers and tipsters. (vg) £6 - £8

▲ **Shot glass.** Commemorating Oxo's win in 1959. Circa 1970. (vg) £4 - £6

The first running of the Epsom Derby was in 1780. It is now Britain's most valuable horserace. The race is watched on television by millions across the world. This ensures plenty of interest with collectors of memorabilia. Racecards, particularly pre-1935 are in demand. Items from any year, signed by the winning jockey, are also of interest.

▲ **Derby Day racecard from 1979**. Signed by winning jockey Willie Carson (Troy). Also signed by Pat Eddery. Clear, blue ink. No dedication. (g-vg) £10 - £15

▲ **Galtee More**. Derby winner 1897. Wrench Series postcard. Postmarked Manchester 1906. (f-g) £12 - £14

▲ **Huntley and Palmers empty biscuit tin**. Derby Day. 260 x 195 x 80mm. (1935) £16 - £20

▲ **Derby Sweepstake ticket**. Top Ten Promotions. 1966. (g) £1 - £3

▲ Hurst Park 1958. (vg) £20 - £24

▲ Ascot (Stand) 1989. (vg-ex) £6 - £8

▲ Kempton Park 1957. (vg-ex) £14 - £18

▲ Sandown Park 1986. (ex) £6 - £8

▲ Goodwood 1980. (vg) £6 - £8

▲ Newmarket 1993. (vg-ex) £5 - £7

▲ Ludlow 2001. (ex) £7 - £9

▲ Ascot (Stand) 1995. (vg) £4 - £6

▲ **Ludlow 19 Nov. 1938**. (f-g) £14 - £16

▲ **Ascot 25 July 1998**. (g-vg) £1 - £2

▲ **Cheltenham 19 Oct**. 1988. (vg) £1 - £2

▲ **Kempton Park 14 June 1989**. (vg) £1 - £3

▲ **Haydock Park 2 Dec. 1939**. (Gent). (g) £15 - £20

▲ **Newbury 11 Nov. 1987**. (f-g) £1 - £2

▲ **Hereford. 14 Dec. 1990**. (vg) £1 - £3

▲ **Wolverhampton. 25 Jan 1985**. (g-vg) £1 - £2

▲ **Worcester 14 Nov. 1990**. (g-vg) £1 - £2

▲ **Goodwood. 31 Jul 1968**. (vg) £3 - £4

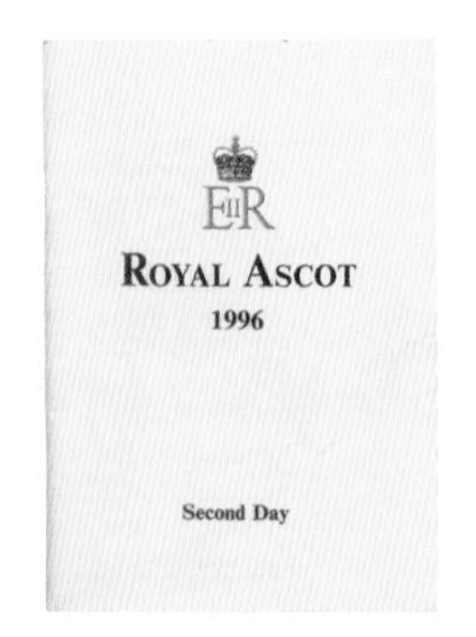

▲ **Royal Ascot. 19 Jun 1996**. (g) £2 - £4

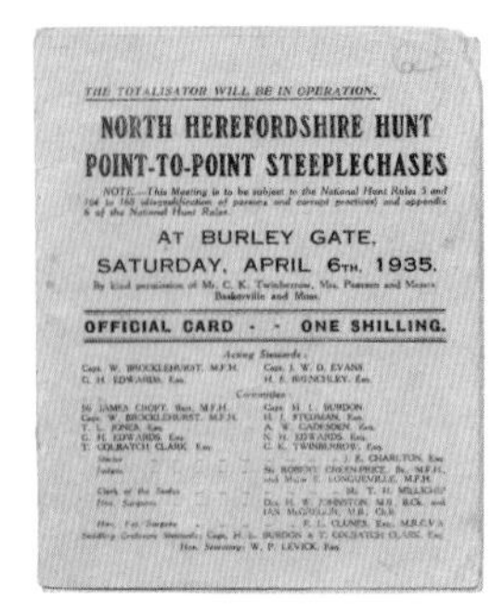

▲ **North Herefordshire. 6 Apr 1935**. (f) £5 - £7

▲ **Folkestone. 10 Jun 1968**. (g) £2 - £3

▲ **Ayr. 22 Sep 1967**. (vg) £2 - £4

▲ **York. 20 Jul 1963**. (g) £2 - £4

▲ **Cheltenham Gold Cup. 15 Mar 1979**. (vg) £2 - £4

▲ **Cheltenham Gold Cup. 15 Mar 1984**. (g) £2 - £4

▲ **Towcester. 26 May 1947**. (vg) £3 - £5

◀ **Newmarket**. Card Game. Universal Publications. Original box and instructions. (1935). (vg) £6 - £8

▲ **Champion Red Rum - Len Marten**. 45rpm single. 1975. Jet Records, JET 753. Vinyl (g) £4 - £6

▲ **Race Fixtures booklet**. 1969. Captain Alan Carfax (racing tipster). (vg) £2 - £3

▲ **Racing Fixtures**. Booklet. 100 x 65mm. Daily Herald. 1936. (g) £5 - £8

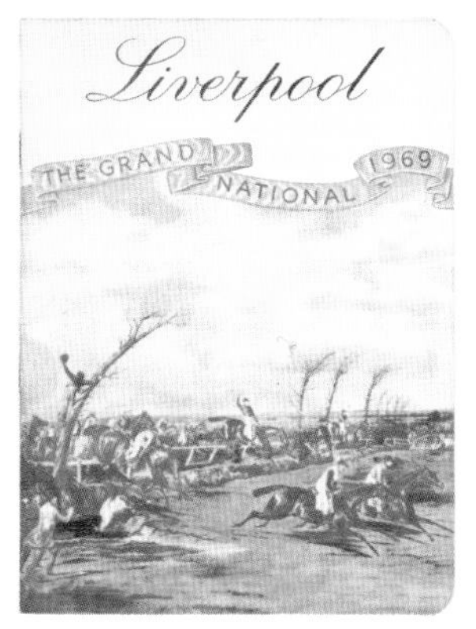

▲ **Race card**. 1969. Highland Wedding was the winner. (g) £2 - £4

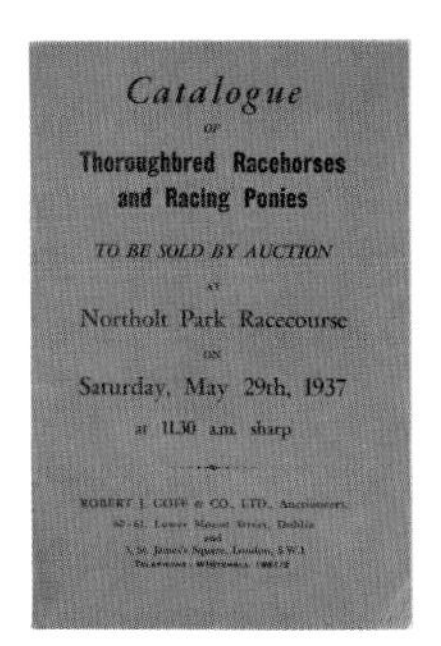
Catalogue
of
Thoroughbred Racehorses
and Racing Ponies
TO BE SOLD BY AUCTION
at
Northolt Park Racecourse
on
Saturday, May 29th, 1937
at 11.30 a.m. sharp

▲ **Goff's Racehorse** Auction Catalogue. 1937. (vg) £8 - £10

▲ **Stable razor blade**. (1950). (vg) £2 - £4

▲ **Derby razor blade**. (1950). (vg) £2 - £4

Football Betting

Arguably, the heyday of the Football Pools was the period 1950 - 1980. The subsequent decline was not helped when the National Lottery came on the scene. Nowadays, it's the poor relation to the Lottery, unable to compete with the prize money offered in Lotto or EuroMillions.

However, there are still plenty of football bets that offer good entertainment value. Mathematically, they rarely offer value for money because the odds are structured by the bookmakers to create a profit for them, not for punters.

Coral's 'The Football Jackpot' and The Football Pools' 'Premier 10' offer bets where you select home, away or draw from a set of specified matches. Whilst the payouts bear no comparison to the lottery, they are good fun. You can make just one, two or three choices. The quantity of selections for each match are multiplied together to determine the cost of the entry. So, if you just made one selection from each of the ten matches at a £1 unit stake your bet would be 1x1x1x1x1x1x1x1x1x1 = 1 x £1 = £1. The following example was an actual 'Big Divi' syndicate winning jackpot entry for Saturday, 21 December 2013 with The Football Pools' 'Premier 10':-

	Home Team	Result	Away Team	Big Divi Entry Home win	Draw	Away win
1.	Man Utd	**3-1**	West Ham	✓		
2.	Crystal Palace	**0-3**	Newcastle		✓	✓
3.	Fulham	**2-4**	Man City			✓
4.	Liverpool	**3-1**	Cardiff	✓		
5.	Southampton	**2-3**	Tottenham	✓	✓	✓
6.	Stoke	**2-1**	Aston Villa	✓	✓	✓
7.	Sunderland	**0-0**	Norwich		✓	✓
8.	Swansea	**1-2**	Everton			✓
9.	West Brom	**1-1**	Hull	✓	✓	✓
10.	Burnley	**2-1**	Blackpool	✓	✓	

The jackpot-winning Big Divi 'Premier 10' entry for 21 December 2013

1x2x1x1x3x3x2x1x3x2 = 216 x £1 = £216 staked.

A good tip to help you win this bet is to remember that the mathematical chance of a football match ending in a draw after ninety minutes of play is LESS than a home win or an away win.

If you assume that on average most matches are likely to fall within the boundaries of no more than three goals being scored by either side, then the percentage chances of each of the three possible outcomes are as follows:-

HOME	37.5%
AWAY	37.5%
DRAW	25%

Football match results cannot be forecast with certainty and indeed many results go against Club form. It may pay to be brave and select a home win and an away win when the form book indicates the likelihood of a draw and where an away win is the popular choice, go for a home selection, on the basis that the home team will have the advantage of the home crowd support. By backing against the popular choice, you are more likely to scoop a bigger payout if you have to share the jackpot.

Coral's 'The Football Jackpot' offers bigger dividends than The Football Pools' 'Premier 10', but the chances of winning are longer. The Premier 10 bet has 10 matches and the The Football Jackpot bet has 15 matches.

The National Lottery Lotto

The National Lottery has been a resounding success for the Government. It has also proved to be popular with the public. Unfortunately, it hasn't provided the majority of us with an easy route to a small fortune. This section aims to explain and explore methods of improving the winning possibilities. Above all, the Lotto must be considered as an entertainment, rather than a serious chance to make a profit or become hugely wealthy overnight.

The Romans were the originators of lotteries. They were devised for very similar reasons that our own Lotto was created. Nero and friends found lotteries an ideal method of creating revenue.

The National Lottery launched in November 1994 was not the first for Britain. The very first dated back to the year 1566 when Queen Elizabeth I was on the throne. The revenue helped pay the costs of the Navy. Lotteries in Britain were popular throughout the centuries and they even paid for the building of The British Museum and Westminster Bridge. It all came to a sticky end when it was alleged that Government officials were corrupt and in 1826 the Government banned all lotteries.

Britain was the last of the European countries to adopt a modern-day National Lottery. Think of the revenue this lethargy has cost!

There's no doubt whatsoever, when Camelot launched the National Lottery in November 1994, the British public welcomed it with unparalleled enthusiasm. In fact it instantly became the largest single lottery in the world. Predictably, the novelty factor quickly wore off as queuing became a chore for many and lack of a win in those early draws did nothing to boost popularity. Nevertheless, the National Lottery (now called Lotto) is still incredibly well supported and looks likely to be with us forever. Many Lotto players now buy their tickets online.

The Lotto game was launched with 49 numbers for players to select from and remained so for the first 21 years. In October 2015, the Lotto game changed to allow players 59 numbers to select from. The extra ten numbers have meant the chances of matching the jackpot winning line have been made significantly worse. At the same time, extra prizes were introduced to keep players interested.

No matter what you may be told, there is no secret method of winning the Lotto OTHER THAN by conventional means. In other words, when you buy one or more tickets, you have exactly the same chance as anyone else who has 'invested' the same sum as you.

You can IMPROVE your chance of winning a LARGER SHARE of a jackpot by avoiding the most popular numbers. Numbers between 1 and 31 are more likely to be chosen because so many people link their number selections to family birth dates. So, if there's an abundance of winning numbers between 32 and 59 there's a stronger possibility that a jackpot would be shared by fewer people than an abundance of winning numbers between 1 and 31.

'Nice' numbers should also be avoided, as they are likely to be chosen by the masses and therefore the chances of the jackpot having to be shared, increase. 'Nice' numbers are; 1, 3, 7, 8, 10, 11, 17, 18, 20, 21, 22, 30, 33, 40, 44. Some may argue that '13' should be included on the basis that it is a notoriously 'unlucky' number. Mathematically it has just the same chance of coming up as any other number, but if people avoid it in large enough quantities, then when it does come up, fewer people are likely to share the prize money and the dividend rises, (other than the 'three numbers correct' £25 prize).

Statistically, your chance of winning the jackpot is a cool 45,057,474 to 1 for a single ticket. However, if you normally purchase 1 ticket a week but instead purchased 10 tickets (all with a different set of six numbers), your chance of winning the jackpot dramatically improves, although still an outrageous 4,505,747 to 1. It can be argued that by selecting six numbers and watching them in the draw for nine weeks, WITHOUT putting your money on, you get far better value if you then spend all the £20 buying 10 tickets on the tenth week. We call this THE PATIENT PLAYER SYSTEM. You do need to be a rather bold player. Just think how sick you would feel if you came up with a winning line of six numbers during your nine weeks ‘rest’ period! For those not so brave, you can simply wait nine weeks then place ten times your normal weekly stake on the tenth week, but make sure you select a whole new set of numbers each time you buy the tickets, that way, you cannot know which numbers you would have played in the 'rest period'. Not playing for nine weeks out of ten will of course spoil much of the fun, nevertheless, it is a REALISTIC and mathematically proven method of improving your chances of winning, in a single draw.

Buying ten £2 Lotto tickets for one draw also considerably improves your chances of winning a smaller prize. The odds reduce to 9.7-1 that you will match a 3-number line and win a £25 prize. There is an even greater chance that you will match a 2-number line and win a free go on a Lucky Dip ticket. This could, in turn, give you the chance of winning a large money prize. However, if you started to think about TRYING to win a smaller prize then you would be far better off placing your £20 on the horses. A £20 win bet on a winning Evens chance would return you £40 AND you would have a genuinely far better chance of winning, especially if there were no more than six runners in the horse race (true odds would be 5-1 of you selecting the winner). BETTER STILL, if you choose a 5-1 chance in a six horse race (rather than a 1-2 hot favourite), you get superb value for money, compared with the Lotto.

Taking the Lotto multiple stake system one step further, by joining a syndicate that will buy 100 tickets for one draw, you seriously improve your chance of sharing a decent return, particularly with the FIVE MAIN NUMBERS PLUS THE BONUS NUMBER.

The odds are reduced from 7,509,579 - 1, to 75,096 - 1. Admittedly the prize fund then has to be shared, but that could be as much as £200,000 shared between 100 = £2,000 each.

If 1,000 people shared a jackpot of £5million, each would receive £5,000. OK it's not the same as winning a sum that will enable you to retire, but it's still a very worthwhile prize.

Never mind if you have never had the slightest interest in the subject of mathematics. The Lottery is a game of chance. In mathematical terms, it is governed by the Laws of Chance. Galileo (Italian Mathematician 1564 - 1642) was consulted by gamblers for assistance. In 1620 he came up with the first clear exposition on the Laws of Chance. It is truly fascinating to delve into Galileo's theories and interpret all he is saying in lottery terms.

In simple terms; When an event (the Lotto, for example) can have more than one result (it could in fact be any one of 45,057,474 results), if all the POSSIBLE results have an equal chance of occurring (which they do, because there is no bias in the selection of the six numbers and the bonus number), then the PROBABILITY of any one of them occurring in a single trial (one Saturday night draw), will be the proportion which that particular result bears to all the possible results.

The law of chance deals with PROPORTIONATE LAW and it's quite likely that you will not be familiar with it. However, it is very likely that you WILL be familiar with the LAW OF AVERAGES. Yet an analysis of this Law confirms that it will be of little real benefit in Lotto terms, simply because you would need to be around for hundreds of years to glean any advantage and even then, it's all rather vague.

The Law of Averages states:- Whenever something can have more than one result, if all the possible results have an equal chance of occurring, the results that will be observed in a number of trials will generally vary to some extent from the inherent proportions, but the extent of this variation will become progressively less as the number of trials is increased.

In other words, whilst the PROBABILITY of any particular number being drawn is no greater or less than any other, the Law of Averages states that there is LIKELY to be an even spread of all of the numbers, given a long enough sequence of draws. Realistically you could expect an even spread in a sample of about 5000 draws. However, given that there are only two Lotto per week or 104 draws a year, you would need to analyse about 48 years worth of results to establish a pattern.

Now, granted the fact that a pattern of equality is likely to evolve, you could attempt to predict the balance of equality as a system for choosing your Lotto numbers. Whereas it is unlikely to seriously improve your chances, because there is mathematical acceptance of the Law of Averages, you should find this system as good as any. So you simply choose numbers that haven't been coming up so much as others.

Some mathematicians have spent countless hours trying to prove a bias in the machinery and balls used in various other countries' lotteries. However, one must seriously doubt that such equipment would be anything other than 'true'. A bias discovered in any of the balls would quickly be discovered by the organisers in test draws. Casinos are constantly monitoring roulette bias (it's the very last thing they need), equally you can be assured that Camelot will be very much aware of the necessity to monitor bias. One 'expert observer' has claimed that a bias does exist in the weight of the balls, because the amount of paint used for the numbers on the balls, will vary. However, there is a tiny chance (although extremely remote) that a bias exists in the National Lottery equipment and following patterns and sequences would at least be as good a method as any for selecting numbers.

If you are lucky enough to win a million or more, then be prepared for a few problems. Apart from the long lost friends crawling out of the woodwork, you could have the media pursuing you. A psychologist may also come in useful. So could an accountant and a lawyer. If you think you would carry on working despite your good fortune, forget it, a fortune will change your life, that's a fact. You might become so suspicious of your friends that you will possibly decide to move to a new area and start your new life amongst other wealthy people. You might even regret the winning of a fortune and yearn for a return to 'normal' life amongst 'real' people.

The price of entering the National Lottery should be assessed in true cost terms. You are far better off joining a syndicate (no matter how big or small) provided (a) you can trust the organiser and (b) you are not the person who is responsible for visiting and paying the National Lottery outlet or spending too long collecting each player's stakes.

If you have to travel SPECIFICALLY to a National Lottery outlet to place your entry, the cost of the travel should be taken into consideration and particularly the amount of time you take to do the travelling and to queue up to place the entry. It is far from inconceivable that 15 minutes would be spent in such activities. If you then translate that time into time worked at £8 per hour, your entry has in theory cost a further £2 to place. If you spent further money on specific travel, then again you could probably add another £1. Time and administration spent on collecting stakes from syndicate players, is also worth consideration.

Inflation over the years will mean that the cost of buying a single ticket will reduce in real terms. However, the value of the smaller prizes also reduces. The winning factor in this argument is the jackpot. The fact that £2million is worth less than it was ten years ago isn't going to worry the winner one iota. So, whilst the cost of a single ticket remains at £2, the deal gets better and better, as long as inflation continues to rise.

Retailers receive a 5% commission for selling tickets.

THE ODDS OF WINNING THE MAIN LOTTO GAME (from 59 Lotto numbers)		
	TRUE ODDS	**APPROXIMATE PAYOUT**
2 main numbers matched	10.3-1	Free Lotto Lucky Dip
3 main numbers matched	97-1	£25
4 main numbers matched	2,180-1	£100
5 main numbers matched	144,415-1	£1,000
5 main numbers matched + bonus	7,509,579-1	£50,000
Jackpot - 6 main numbers matched	45,057,474-1	£Jackpot

Rollover Value

Watch out for ROLLOVER draws. These can represent better value for money because the top prizes can be boosted considerably. From October 2015, there will be no maximum number of Rollovers. The jackpot could continue to roll until it reaches or exceeds a pre-agreed amount (determined by the National Lottery). Once the jackpot has reached this pre-agreed amount, it can only rollover once more before it must be won. If nobody matches the jackpot line in that next Lotto draw, the entire jackpot amount will roll down to the next prize tier which has at least one winner.

On the draw when the jackpot prize must be won i.e. at the point a roll down could occur, this represents a better value for money draw to enter.

Obviously, if the jackpot prize does roll down to the next prize tier, e.g. 5 Main numbers plus the Bonus number, there are likely to be more winners at this 'lower' level. However, even if the roll down jackpot has to be shared between several winning tickets, there's a good chance that each winning ticket could be worth a 6-figure sum.

Lotto Hotpicks

Lotto Hotpicks was introduced in early 2002 under a blaze of publicity. You could be forgiven for believing that the massive advertising campaign was designed to make Hotpicks appear to be a far better value game than the traditional £25 payout for selecting three correct numbers from the Lotto draw. The promise of £800 for getting three numbers correct, could, to some people, appear to be a fantastic opportunity.

Being able to win by getting just two numbers correct, may also seem to be very attractive. Particularly as so many people regularly manage to get two numbers correct from the main six numbers drawn. The National Lottery blurb said 'win big prizes by picking and matching fewer numbers'. In fact, the two games have completely different mathematical calculations, the two games do not compare, even though the same six numbers are being used for Hotpicks and the main Lotto game.

There is a huge difference in ANY two or three numbers from six (the Lotto game) and two or three SPECIFIC numbers from six (the Hotpicks game). The calculation to determine the true chance of selecting two SPECIFIC numbers is 59 x 58 = 3422 divided by 6 x 5 (= 30) = 114, or approximately 114-1. However, the actual payout is a mere 59-1 (£60 including £1 returned stake).

Hotpicks is more of a fixed odds bet than a lottery and represents very poor value (paying only about 50% of the true odds). Fortunately, those punters who understand the mathematics of it all, will recognise the shortcomings.

Take a look at the odds a casino pays out if you correctly select just one number from a possible 37 numbers (1 - 36, plus 0). The true odds are 36-1 but the casino pays a handsome 35-1. The value is there for all to see and endorses what an incredibly poor value bet Hotpicks is.

The true odds for 3 specific numbers from 59 is 1,625-1, Hotpicks only pays 799-1. The true odds for 4 specific numbers from 59 is 30,341-1, Hotpicks only pays 12,999-1.

Moreover, in the Lotto Hotpicks game, you have the option to play Pick 1, Pick 2, Pick 3, Pick 4, or Pick 5. If you choose to play Pick 4, for example, and choose say 7, 15, 21 and 29, but only 7, 15 and 29 come up in the main Lotto draw, you cannot win the Pick 4 prize because you obviously didn't match all four numbers, but unlike the Lotto, you will not even win the lower prize category for matching three numbers. However, in the Lotto you would still win the prize for matching three numbers and would (normally) win £25.

Another National Lottery run game is the Thunderball.

The Thunderball top prize is £500,000 and this is won by correctly choosing five Main Numbers (from 1 to 34) plus the 'Thunderball' number (from 1 to 14). Because there are less balls, the chance of winning this smaller jackpot is greater than for the Lotto itself, but the winnings are paid at fixed odds and still do not represent good value for money.

EuroMillions

In addition, you can play EuroMillions which can offer a huge jackpot prize, often far greater than the Lotto itself, as it is played in several different countries within the EU.

EuroMillions is played by France, Spain, United Kingdom, Belgium, Austria, Ireland, Luxembourg, Portugal and Switzerland, with more European countries looking to join. It's played on both Tuesday and Friday evenings each week.

Costing the same price as the Lotto at £2 per ticket, yet often offering a greater jackpot, you can see why so many people play it.

Since introducing the prize level for matching just two numbers from the 10th May 2011, there has been a huge surge in the number of EuroMillions winners. Now, there are 14 levels of prizes in the EuroMillions, which has attracted a lot of players. The odds of matching two numbers is 1 in 23, which seems easy, so why not try it? Who knows, you might match all 5 Main numbers and 2 Lucky Star numbers instead.

The biggest EuroMillions Jackpot that was ever won was for Draw Number 510 on Friday 10th August 2012. The lucky ticket holders, Adrian and Gillian Bayford from Suffolk, pocketed an impressive 190 million Euros (£148 million). Due to differences in the exchange rate, the largest single Sterling winner of the EuroMillions came from the draw on the 12th July 2011 and was won by Christine and Colin Weir from Largs in Scotland, who scooped a massive £161,653,000 (185 million Euros).

However, as you would expect for a Europe-wide lottery, the EuroMillions jackpot is a very difficult one to win. In order to scoop the top prize you must match five Main numbers plus two Lucky Star Numbers. The chance of doing so is an astronomical 1 in 116,531,800 and even to match five Main Numbers and one Lucky Star Number is a 1 in 6,473,989 chance. Still, even these odds are not enough to put off those chasing a dream jackpot that would literally change their lives, and those of their friends and family, forever.

Lottery Facts and Trivia

- **In the first month of operation, 206 million Lotto tickets were sold, 3.5 million people shared £100 million prize money but only thirty-five people won more than £100,000 each and just five people won more than £1million.**
- Only 50% of the total sum of Lotto tickets purchased is paid out in prize money. The remaining 50% is distributed as follows; 10% in operating costs, 5% to the retailer, 12% to the Government (tax) and 23% to good causes (Arts, Sport, Charity and others).
- **The balls used in the Lotto draw machines are made of solid rubber.**
- An 84-year-old widow from Florida, America became the winner of the biggest ever jackpot at £383million in the Powerball in June 2013.
- **By Law, no person under the age of sixteen years is permitted to partake in UK lotteries.**
- The biggest ever EuroMillions jackpot win was in August 2012, when a couple from Suffolk scooped €190million (£148million).
- **The £17.8 million winner of the Lotto in December 1994, who requested anonymity, instantly became the 1,500th richest person in Britain.**
- Due to differences in exchange rates, the largest pound sterling jackpot win came in July, 2011, when a couple from Largs, Scotland won an incredible £161,653,000 on the EuroMillions game.
- **In 2002, Camelot changed the name of the National Lottery to Lotto.**
- Anne Morgan of Colyford, Devon, had a dream about the lottery numbers. When she awoke, she wrote the numbers down. She scooped a win of £337,644.
- **National Lottery players have so far raised an unbelievable £34billion for good causes.**
- Former cleaner Dolores McNamara from Limerick, Ireland, won £79million on the Euromillions lottery.

The Lottery Club

The Lottery Club began over 20 years ago. It was originally designed to complement the Elite Racing Club service. The concept was (and still is) that a thousand or more people would club together to play the Saturday Lotto game.

In 2013 The Lottery Club became part of Big Divi (see page 115).

The weekly newsletter is posted to all subscribers keeping everyone up-to-date with all the latest lottery news and the syndicate's winnings.

The best win that The Lottery Club has achieved (at the time of writing) is £250,000, when 5 Main numbers plus the Bonus ball were matched.

There have been numerous jackpot near misses where five numbers have been matched and the remaining number has been really close to the winning one.

EuroMillions and Thunderball have now been added to The Lottery Club syndicate.

The Lottery Club is believed to be the longest established large syndicate of its kind in the United Kingdom.

If you like the idea of joining a big syndicate then details can be found on the website: **www.bigdivi.co.uk** or telephone **01380 811700** or write to: **Big Divi, P.O.Box 100, Devizes, SN10 4TE**.

Lotto - The Conclusion

Buying a £2 ticket is, in reality, **not a good value for money bet**, given the long odds against winning the jackpot. However, it does represent value 'entertainment wise'. Every draw is YOUR CHANCE to scoop a large sum of money and, let's face it, people DO win. It is this belief that you COULD be one of the lucky ones, that makes it so exciting. By joining a syndicate, you improve your chances of being a WINNER, no matter how small the sum and that's a thrill. It would be fair to say that if the draw was not shown LIVE on television, the entertainment value would be considerably reduced.

Basically, one must conclude that the National Lottery needs to be treated as a bit of fun and there is, of course, the consolation that part of the cost of each ticket goes to a good cause.

A Racing Chronology

1660 Charles II and his court patronised horseracing at Newmarket.

1689 The Byerley Turk, a stallion brought to England by Captain Robert Byerley, began the scientific breeding of the thoroughbred race horse.

1704 Breeder Richard Darley imported a stallion from Syria (The Darley Arabian) and became responsible for two of the greatest thoroughbreds of all time, Eclipse and Flying Childers.

1711 Ascot Racecourse founded by command of Queen Anne.

1727 The first Racing Calendar was published (by John Cheney of Arundel).

1751 The Jockey Club was founded by enthusiasts.

1752 Horses raced a distance between parish churches, from steeple to steeple, creating the first steeplechase.

1757 Herod was bred by The Duke of Cumberland. Many Classic winners can be traced back to this stallion.

1758 Jockeys were required to weigh-in after a race.

1762 Racing colours first registered.

1763 Richard Tattersall organised first bloodstock sale, at Hyde Park in London.

1773 The Weatherby family took over The Racing Calendar.

1776 The St. Leger was founded, and was therefore the first Classic race run.

1779 Bridget wins the first running of The Oaks.

1780 The first running of The Derby, won by Sir Charles Bunbury's Diomed.

1791 The General Stud Book first published.

1797 Rules of Racing published for the first time.

1807 Master Jackey wins the first running of The Ascot Gold Cup.

1809 Wizard wins the first running of the 2,000 Guineas.

1810 Australia's first official race meeting was held.

1814 Charlotte wins the first running of the 1,000 Guineas.

1822 Middleham trainer James Croft saddled the first four home in the St Leger.

1835 The first official list of Jockey Club members published.

1838 Handicapper Admiral Rous was first made a Steward of The Jockey Club.

1839 First running of The Grand National.

1840 First running of Goodwood's Stewards' Cup.

1843 First running of The Ebor Handicap at York.

1844 Running Rein won The Derby, but was later exposed as a four-year old 'ringer'. The race was awarded to Orlando.

1845 Henry Wright devised the first Steeplechasing Calendar.

1853 Betting and Gaming Act made cash betting off-course illegal.

1859 Jockey Club banned the racing of yearlings.

1859 Mayonnaise won the 1,000 Guineas by 20 lengths.

1861 First running of The Melbourne Cup.

1866 The Irish Derby was run for the first time.

1866 National Hunt Committee formed by The Jockey Club.

1870 First running of The Irish Grand National.

1874 Fred Archer won his first of 13 consecutive Flat Champion Jockey titles.

1874 The first running of the Velka Pardubice in the country formerly known as Czechoslovakia.

1875 First enclosed racecourse in England is opened at Sandown Park.

1877 Draw for places at the start of a race became a Jockey Club rule.

1879 Jockeys are required to be licensed.

1886 Fred Archer committed suicide at the height of his career, aged 29.

1891 Bookmaking became illegal in France and from then on betting be came restricted to the Pari-Mutuel.

1900 Diamond Jubilee won The Derby. This was owner King Edward VII's second Derby win after Persimmon triumphed in 1896.

1902 Sceptre won every Classic race barring the Derby, only failing by a narrow margin to be the only horse in history to win all five Classic races.

1904 Pretty Polly won the Oaks at odds of 8-100.

1905 National Hunt racing at Newmarket ended.

1907 Orby became the first Irish-trained horse to win The Derby.

1909 King Edward VII won The Derby for the third and final time with Minoru.

1914 Steve Donoghue became Champion Flat Jockey and retained the title for ten years.

1916 The Grand National was held at Gatwick, Surrey.

1920 Number cloths introduced.

1924 First running of The Cheltenham Gold Cup.

1925 Gordon Richards won his first of 26 Champion Flat Jockey titles.

1926 Betting tax introduced by Winston Churchill, then Chancellor of the Exchequer.

1927 First running of The Champion Hurdle.

1928 The Tote was instituted by Act of Parliament.

1928 Australian jockey Scobie Breasley rode his first winner in Melbourne.

1929 Betting tax abolished.

1929 A record field of 66 runners contested The Grand National.

1930 Run-offs no longer staged for dead-heats.

1932 Golden Miller won his first of five consecutive Cheltenham Gold Cups.

1933 Gordon Richards beats Fred Archer's record of riding 248 winners in a season.

1933 Hyperion won The Derby and St. Leger.

1939 Fred Rimell won his first of four Champion Jump Jockey titles at the age of 26.

1942 World War II halts National Hunt racing for two years.

1947 First evening meeting held, at Hamilton Park.

1948 Cottage Rake won his first of three Cheltenham Gold Cups.

1948 Peter O'Sullevan made his first broadcast on BBC Radio.

1949 Mirabel Topham bought Aintree racecourse for £275,000.

1951 Jockey Edward Hide rode his first of 2,591 winners.

1953 Huge betting scam on Frascal at Bath. Four gang members jailed.

1953 Fred Winter won first of four National Hunt champion jockey titles.

1953 Jockey Bill Shoemaker (USA) created a world record by riding 485 winners in a year.

1954 Dick Francis became champion jump jockey.

1954 Lester Piggott (aged 18) won his first Derby, on board the 33-1 chance Never Say Die, and the Triumph Hurdle on Prince Charlemagne on the only occasion he rode at The Cheltenham Festival.

1955 Lester Piggott joined Noel Murless as stable jockey.

1956 The Queen Mother's Devon Loch, ridden by Dick Francis, collapsed just a few yards from the winning post, having had the Grand National at his mercy.

1957 The Whitbread Gold Cup became the first commercially sponsored race.

1958 Lord Oaksey OBE (then known as Hon. John Lawrence) became champion amateur National Hunt jockey.

1959 Petite Etoile won the 1,000 Guineas and The Oaks.

1959 Jockey Manny Mercer (elder brother of Joe) was killed instantly when thrown from his mount at Ascot.

1960 The first live television transmission of The Grand National.

1960 Legendary and thoroughly eccentric racing owner Miss Dorothy Paget dies aged 54, having owned numerous winners such as Golden Miller and tormented many trainers in her lifetime by contacting them at all hours of the day and night.

1961 Betting shops legalised and The Levy Board founded to collect a percentage of turnover for the benefit of racing.

1962 Creggmore Boy (aged 22) became the oldest racehorse to compete in a race when running at Cartmel.

1963 Scobie Breasley won his fourth jockey championship.

1963 Mill House won The Cheltenham Gold Cup.

1964 Arkle won the first of three consecutive Cheltenham Gold Cups.

1965 Starting stalls introduced.

1965 Legendary Australian trainer Bart Cummings won the first of eleven Melbourne Cups.

1966 Norah Wilmot became the first lady trainer to win a race, successfully saddling her filly, Pat, at Brighton.

1966 Vincent O'Brien won his first champion trainer title.

1966 Betting tax re-introduced by James Callaghan, Chancellor of the Exchequer.

1967 100-1 outsider, Foinavon won The Grand National.

1967 Park Top (£525 bargain superstar) won her first of 13 races.

1968 Persian War wins the first of three consecutive Champion Hurdles.

1970 John Francome began his riding career with a winner at Worcester aboard Multigrey.

1970 Nijinsky won the Triple Crown (The 2,000 Guineas, the Derby and the St. Leger).

1970 Alexandra Park closes, having been London's most central racecourse.

1971 Brigadier Gerard wins the 2,000 Guineas in a career that sees him beaten only once.

1971 Bula won the first of two consecutive Champion Hurdles.

1971 Fred Winter won his first of eight champion National Hunt trainer titles.

1972 The Jockey Club permitted ladies to ride on the Flat. The first race was The Goya Stakes at Kempton, won by Meriel Tufnell on Scorched Earth.

1972 Stan Mellor became the first National Hunt jockey to ride 1,000 winners.

1973 Mrs.Topham sold Aintree racecourse for £3 million, plunging the future of the track into doubt.

1973 Red Rum won the first of two consecutive Grand Nationals.

1974 Peter Walwyn became champion Flat trainer.

1975 Pat Eddery won his first Derby on Grundy.

1975 Jenny Pitman trains her first winner, Biretta.

1976 H M The Queen Mother enjoyed her 300th National Hunt winner with Sunyboy at Ascot.

1976 Sir Noel Murless retired and handed over his Warren Place Newmarket stables to son-in-law Henry Cecil.

1976 Muriel Naughton became the first female jockey to be permitted to ride in a steeplechase, under Rules.

1976 Diana Thorne (later married to trainer Nicky Henderson) became the first lady jockey to win a National Hunt Race.

1977 Red Rum won The Grand National for the third and final time.

1977 Charlotte Brew became the first lady jockey to ride in The Grand National.

1977 The Queen's Dunfermline won the Oaks and St. Leger.

1977 Lanark racecourse closed.

1978 John Francome won The Cheltenham Gold Cup on Midnight Court.

1979 Willie Carson won his first Derby on Troy.

1981 Shergar won The Derby by a record ten lengths.

1981 Aldaniti won The Grand National, ridden by former cancer sufferer Bob Champion.

1981 Teeside Park racecourse closed.

1983 Jenny Pitman became the first woman to train the winner of The Grand National with Corbiere.

1983 Trainer Michael Dickinson saddled the first five horses home in the Cheltenham Gold Cup.

1983 Brilliant Derby winner, Shergar, was kidnapped from Stud, possibly by the IRA. He was never to be seen again, his whereabouts has been much discussed, but is assumed to have been a bungled ransom plot.

1984 Mare Dawn Run won The Champion Hurdle.

1984 Steve Cauthen became the first American jockey to win the Flat jockeys' championship since Danny Maher (1913).

1984 Jenny Pitman became the first woman to train a Cheltenham Gold Cup winner with Burrough Hill Lad.

1985 Lester Piggott retired, for the first time.

1985 John Francome retired as a jockey.

1986 Mare Dawn Run won The Cheltenham Gold Cup.

1986 HRH Princess Anne won her first race as a jockey.

1987 Gay Kelleway became the first woman jockey to ride a winner at Royal Ascot on Sprowston Boy.

1987 Lester Piggott was convicted of tax evasion.

1987 HRH Princess Anne won a steeplechase riding her own horse, Cnoc No Cuille.

1987 S.I.S. (Satellite Information Services) began their transmission of televised racing into betting shops.

1988 Kribensis gave leading Flat owner Sheikh Mohammed his first Cheltenham Festival winner, winning The Triumph Hurdle.

1989 Martin Pipe won his first Champion National Hunt trainer's title with 208 winners.

1989 Desert Orchid won the Cheltenham Gold Cup, despite atrocious conditions.

1989 Sunday Silence won The Kentucky Derby and Breeders' Cup Classic. His owner had paid only $17,000 for him. His progeny had won over $323million by the time of his death in 2002.

1990 100-1 outsider, Norton's Coin won The Cheltenham Gold Cup. He was owned and trained by Welsh dairy farmer Sirrell Griffiths.

1990 Lester Piggott came out of retirement and returned to professional race riding when finishing second on Lupesco at Leicester.

1990 Northern Dancer, arguably the greatest thoroughbred stallion of modern times, died at the age of 29.

1991 The brilliant Arazi won The Breeders' Cup Juvenile and $1million.

1992 Desert Orchid was retired.

1993 The British Horseracing Board (BHB) was set up.

1993 Grand National declared void after a shambolic false start. Jockey John White had passed the post first on Esha Ness.

1993 Vintage Crop won The Melbourne Cup, trained by Dermot Weld and ridden by Mick Kinane.

1995 Lammtarra became the first Derby winner to be the produce of Derby and Oaks winners (Nijinsky out of Snow Bride). The start of the rise to prominence of leading global owners, Godolphin, headed by Sheikh Mohammed.

1995 Red Rum died and was buried next to the winning post at Aintree racecourse.

1995 The Derby was moved from being run on a Wednesday to a Saturday to make the race meeting more accessible to people that work during the week.

1996 The prolific Cigar won the first Dubai World Cup and 16 consecutive races. He won very nearly $10 m in prize money, but proved infertile when sent to stud.

1996 National Hunt jockey Tony McCoy won his first championship Title.

1997 Kieren Fallon won his first Flat champion jockey title.

1998 Istabraq and Charlie Swan won the first of three consecutive Champion Hurdles.

1998 Alex Greaves became the first female jockey to ride in The Derby.

1998 The popular grey One Man was killed in a fall, having won that season's Champion Chase on his previous start. He had twice failed to make the frame in the Cheltenham Gold Cup.

1999 Jockey Richard Dunwoody retired from the saddle, having won 1,699 races.

1999 Trainer Jenny Pitman retired, her last winner being Scarlet Emperor at Huntingdon.

2000 A plane crash at Newmarket killed the pilot and injured jockeys Frankie Dettori and Ray Cochrane. The latter retired from race-riding later that year.

2000 The hard working Kevin Darley became champion Flat jockey.

2000 The phenomenon of Betting Exchanges starts.

2001 Cheltenham Festival lost to Foot and Mouth disease.

2001 Galileo, trained by Aidan O'Brien and ridden by Mick Kinane, won The Derby, before going on to replace his predecessor, Sadler's Wells, as one of the most important modern day stallions in the world.

2001 Betting tax (then at 9%) abolished.

2002 Tony McCoy won the National Hunt jockeys' title with an incredible 289 wins, therefore beating Sir Gordon Richard's record of 269 winners, set in 1933.

2002 Best Mate, ridden by Jim Culloty, won the first of three consecutive Cheltenham Gold Cups. He was later attributed by Tony McCoy as 'the best Gold Cup horse I ever rode.'

2003 Charlie Swan retired from riding. He was Irish champion jockey nine times.

2003 Pat Eddery retires from riding, converting his stud into a training establishment.

2004 Ballinger Ridge, ridden by Kieren Fallon, is narrowly beaten at Lingfield, which starts massive debate about race fixing. Police and Jockey Club investigations began. After a lengthy battle in the High Court, Fallon is cleared some years later and was allowed to continue his riding career.

2005 Hayley Turner became only the fourth female jockey to ride the 95 winners needed to lose her apprentice claim, in doing so sharing the champion apprentice title.

2005 UK senior jockey George Duffield retired after one of the longest stable jockey associations known in the sport (30 years), with Sir Mark Prescott. George rode 2,547 winners and was based at Heath House nearly all his professional career, having begun his apprenticeship with Sir Mark's former employer, Jack Waugh.

2006 Multiple champion jumps trainer Martin Pipe retires the day after the end of the season, when he is beaten by Paul Nicholls for the first time.

2007 Frankie Dettori finally wins his first Derby on favourite Authorized.

2007 Kieren Fallon gives his favourite horse, Dylan Thomas, a superb ride to win the Arc, despite a lengthy stewards' enquiry.

2008 Tony McCoy rides at the Cheltenham Festival just six weeks after breaking vertebrae in his back.

2008 Sir Michael Stoute finally wins his first St Leger with Conduit.

2009 Kauto Star was given a rating of 193 after winning the King George VI Chase at Kempton Park, the highest rating ever given to a chaser.

2009 Three of Sir Michael Stoute's horses: Conduit, Tartan Bearer and Ask finish first, second and third in the King George VI and Queen Elizabeth Diamond Stakes at Ascot

2012 Nicky Henderson trained six winners at the Cheltenham Festival - the most in history.

2013 A P McCoy wins his 4000th race on Mountain Tunes.

2013 Jockey Eddie Ahern banned by the BHA from race riding for 10 years.

2013 Trainers Mahmood Al Zarooni and Gerard Butler are warned off after being found guilty of using steroids on their horses. Each horse that tested positive for illegal steroid was banned from racing for six months, including Al Zarooni's Certify, who was favourite for the 1,000 Guineas at that stage.

2014 The first race meeting to be held under Rules in Great Britain on a Good Friday (18 April 2014). Lingfield was the venue and race prize money for the day amounted to £1million.

2014 Johnny Murtagh retired from the saddle, to concentrate on a training career, having mixed the two for a season.

2015 A P McCoy retires from race riding, having won 20 jockeys' championships in the most astounding career.

2015 Richard Hughes retires from race-riding mid-season to begin his training career, having been champion for the last 3 years.

Racing/Betting Glossary

A

ACCEPTORS This is a term used to include every horse that has stood his ground at a secondary forfeit stage for a big race. The word comes from the owner's acceptance of the horse's handicap mark, which will have been published by the handicapper.

ADDED MONEY Funds added to the race prize money.

AGE OF A RACEHORSE Every racehorse born in the northern hemisphere celebrates its birthday on January 1st every year. For example, if a horse is born in April of one year, he will become a yearling on the following New Year's Day regardless of the fact that he is only eight months old. The following year, he will become a two-year-old, or 'juvenile', and is able to race on the Flat. At three, horses are permitted to race in 'juvenile hurdles', which start in the summer. At four, horses may race over fences in the autumn.

ALL OUT The term used to describe a horse that has been pushed to its maximum at the finish of a race.

ALSO RAN The term given to horses that were not 'placed' in a race.

AMATEUR RIDER These riders are not officially paid to ride in a race in the UK (they are in Ireland), and are identified with the title of 'Mr', 'Miss', 'Mrs,' etc. Amateurs can ride in the same National Hunt races as professionals once they have gained enough experience against other amateurs. They also claim an allowance, and keep theirs for life or until they have ridden out their claim.

APPEAL These are objections lodged with the British Horseracing Authority (BHA) by owners, jockeys or trainers after a result or punishment dealt by race day stewards (see 'Stewards'). The intention of an appeal is to overrule a ban, fine or even change a result imposed by the stewards after a race. The appeal is brought before stewards at a meeting at the BHA's London Headquarters, who will reconsider the offence, and agree whether the discipline dealt was sufficient or harsh and act accordingly. Statistically, appeals rarely tend to change the raceday result as the quality of racecourse stewarding is now so high.

APPRENTICE Every Flat jockey riding as a professional will have started their career as an apprentice. An apprentice must remain with a trainer in full time employment until his claim has been ridden out, which means he has ridden enough winners to no longer receive an allowance. He may then become a freelance jockey. The trainer should guide and educate the apprentice to help their career, and can claim a percentage of their riding fees if desired.

AUCTION MAIDEN These races are for horses that have not won a race and have passed through a public auction at some stage.

AUCTION RACES These are not selling or claiming races, but are for horses (usually juveniles) that have passed through public auction. They are allotted a weight in each race according to their auction purchase price, with the most expensive carrying the most weight.

AUTUMN DOUBLE Two of the Flat season's most competitive Flat handicaps, the Cambridgeshire and the Cesarewitch.

B

BAR 'Except the horses mentioned'. The bookmaker may offer odds for six of the ten runners in the race, but will not quote the final four less fancied horses, stating that they are (e.g.) 20/1 bar, meaning their prices are 20/1 or greater.

BISMARK A fancied horse that a bookmaker does not expect to win on any given day.

BIT A metal steering mechanism that is placed in the horse's mouth. Reins are attached to the bit to provide the jockey with control. Most horses run in 'snaffle' bits, which are linked in the middle of the mouth. Should a horse 'hang' or 'pull', other more severe bits are available to help the jockey steer and control the horse to enhance performance.

BLACK TYPE Black or 'bold' type is printed in the summary of a horse's pedigree if it has been placed in a Pattern race (i.e. a Group, Graded or Listed race). If the horse's name appears in bold type and upper case, it has won a pattern race. If the horse is a filly or mare, its value should increase dramatically, as their progeny will be more attractive to potential purchasers.

BLEEDER A horse that is said to 'bleed' is one that can break blood vessels when racing or working at home. The breaking of blood vessels is caused by a haemorrhage in the lungs, which is can be made apparent by blood appearing in the horse's nostrils. Some horses are very prone to bleeding, which can dramatically hinder their race-winning potential. Some trainers 'scope' (using an endoscope) their horses before they run, to ensure their lungs are free from blood or infection, which will reduce their chances of 'bleeding' under maximum exertion.

BLOWN UP This takes place usually towards the end of a race when a horse cannot run on, usually due to lack of fitness. He is said to have 'blown up' when he has reached his maximum exertion, which is usually earlier in the season if he lacks a recent run to achieve peak condition.

BOARD PRICE This is the price that is shown in betting shops, on television and the internet during the pre-race market. A punter can take the board price advertised at the time, or can bet 'SP' and be paid out at the eventual starting price.

BOOK A bookmaker will open a 'book' on each event that he bets on (hence 'book' maker). A carefully constructed pricing structure devised for a particular event, taking into account betting percentages.

BOTTOMLESS Ground that is extremely heavy and tiring.

B.P.A. The Bookmakers' Protection Association. Founded in 1921 to serve the bookmakers and the betting public, and make sure that both parties have a fair deal.

BREAK DOWN A horse is deemed to have 'broken down' or 'got a leg' when it has damaged a tendon, which can cause him to go lame.

BREAKING IN This is a process that every horse must undergo before he or she can be ridden. The horse is taught to be receptive to the rider's hands and legs. The final stage of the breaking process is to 'back' the horse. A rider is legged up on the horse's back, and then remains leant over the horse until he settles and accepts the rider over his back.

BREEZE UP SALES Young horses are cantered, or 'breezed' past the stands over a few furlongs in front of potential buyers prior to being sold at auction.

BROUGHT DOWN A horse is 'brought down' if he has fallen in a race through no fault of his own, i.e. a horse or jockey has landed in front or baulked the horse causing him to fall.

BUMPER These are ‘National Hunt Flat races’, which are run to educate young horses before they progress to racing over obstacles. Junior Bumpers are run over a mile and four furlongs for three-year-olds, with older horses competing over 1m6f and upwards. Horses must not have run on the Flat or over obstacles. Horses can return to bumpers after running over hurdles in Ireland, assuming they have not won.

'BY' and **'OUT OF'** For breeding purposes, 'by' refers to the sire, and 'out of' refers to his dam. E.g. Soviet Song is BY Marju OUT OF Kalinka.

C

CALENDAR The Racing Calendar is a publication containing details of every race that a trainer or owner may wish to enter their horses in. It is published regularly by Weatherbys.

CARD The race card listing the meeting’s races of the day.

CAST A horse lying down in its stable that is unable to get to its feet, requiring outside assistance. Horses can become injured in this way, as they often panic when stuck.

CERTAINTY A horse thought to be unbeatable. In reality they do not exist, unless there is a one horse race, or 'walkover'.

CHASE A steeplechase. Steeplechasing was named after a match race in 1752 in Ireland, where the finishing post was to be the steeple at St Leger Church.

CLAIMING RACE Each horse entered in a claiming race has a price set by its connections at the 5-day entry stage, and this price then determines the weight the horse will carry. Each horse can be purchased (claimed) after the race for this fee plus a buyer's premium. The owner can also claim his horse back, but is not guaranteed to retain him if other claims are made. Should four claims be received, for example, each interested party has a one in four chance of claiming the horse.

CLASSICS There are five Classic races every Flat racing season, including the 2,000 Guineas and the Derby for colts and fillies and the 1,000 Guineas and the Oaks for fillies alone. The final Classic is the St Leger run for both sexes. The Guineas are run over 1m, the Derby and Oaks over 1m 4f and the St Leger over a 1 m 6 ½ f.

CLASSIFIED STAKES Non-handicaps designed for horses that have run at least three times and/or won a race. They have a rating limit to keep the races competitive.

CLERK OF THE COURSE The person appointed by the racecourse's executive to ensure that the racecourse is well prepared for a day's racing. He must ensure the racecourse is properly marked, the distances are correct, each runner is properly paraded and saddled, each wearing a numbered cloth, and that no disqualified persons are present. The clerk must also act as a public relations officer, ensuring the ground is suitable and an accurate description of the ground condition is published.

COLOURS Every owner must register his racing colours on an annual basis with Weatherbys. Once registered, no one else can use the same colours without permission.

COLIC A severe pain in the abdominal region suffered by a horse. Colic can be caused by a number of reasons, and can be quite serious in horses as they cannot vomit.

COLT An un-castrated male horse aged less than five years.

CONDITION This is the muscular shape of a horse. A horse carrying condition may be very well toned, or may be 'carrying too much condition', which means he may be carrying some excess weight.

CONDITIONAL JOCKEY These are National Hunt apprentices.

CONDITIONS RACES Non-handicap races, but with weight-related conditions attached, generally attracting quite decent horses.

CONFORMATION The shape of a horse's body and limbs.

COVERED UP A horse kept in behind other runners whilst racing, only exposed in the closing stages.

COVERING The process when a stallion mates with a mare. This arrangement generally occurs in the spring in the northern hemisphere, usually from Valentine's Day onwards until the end of May, as most breeders like early foals and precocious horses. A horse's gestation period is eleven months.

CRIB BITER A horse that bites a solid object in its stable, e.g. the door, and draws air back into his throat (a bad habit).

CUT The act of gelding a horse.

CUT IN THE GROUND Rain-softened ground.

DAM The mother of a horse.

DEAD WEIGHT Weight carried on the horse's back in the form of lead when the jockey is lighter than the allotted weight the horse must carry in a race.

DISTANCE A distance of more than thirty lengths between two horses.

DIVIDED RACES If more horses are declared than the racecourse safety factor will permit, then the race may be 'divided' into two. Runners are then split into the two divisions.

DOPE TEST A urine or blood sample taken from a horse after a race. Horses are tested at random, but are usually beaten favourites or high-priced and unexpected winners. The stewards have the right to dope test any horse they choose on a raceday.

DRIFTER A horse discarded by punters in the betting market.

DWELT Starting slowly in a race.

E

EARLY BIRDS Punters who have taken odds offered on horses on the morning of a race.

EARLY DOORS Early morning market exchanges made between punters and bookmakers.

ENTIRE An un-castrated male horse. Also known as a 'full horse'.

ENTRIES & DECLARATIONS Horses are normally entered in races five days in advance. For more prestigious races, there are a series of early closing dates and elimination stages. Horses are usually declared at 10am the day before the race for NH races, and 48 hours before on the Flat. For Sunday racing, all runners must be declared 48 hours in advance.

EUROPEAN BREEDERS' FUND The EBF began in 1983, when breeders gathered together and agreed that a fund should be created, which would include a contribution from stallion owners on an annual basis that is equal to the average covering fee for each sire nominated to the scheme. The result is that only the progeny of the participating stallions would then be eligible for the benefits, as there are a number of EBF races, each being open to EBF registered horses only.

F

FACES Well known characters of the betting ring, acknowledged by bookmakers as being shrewd.

FIELD Runners in a race, form 'the field'.

FILLY A female horse of less than five years of age.

FIRM A going description for turf, which suggests there is little cushion for the horses underfoot.

FIXED BRUSH HURDLES A more solid version of a hurdle, in use at Worcester and Southwell. They have been trialled elsewhere. In Ireland, some courses use 'Easyfix' hurdles, which are made from a solid plastic base, using plastic birch. They are very popular with trainers are can be seen on many training grounds.

FLAGMAN Racecourse employee who stands a short distance from the start of a race, wearing a white coat and carrying a flag which he will wave furiously in front of the runners to signal a false start if necessary.

FOAL A young horse of less than one year of age.

FORFEIT The stage at which a sum becomes payable for a race entry. For instance, races such as the Epsom Derby have several 'forfeit stages', where a fee must be paid to keep the horse entered in the race. Should the fee not be paid, all original entry fees paid for the horse will be 'forfeited'.

FORFEIT LIST The list of persons who have defaulted on financial obligations and thus are barred from running their horses or taking part in racing activities.

FORWARD An early-maturing type of horse. Two-year-olds, who can race as early as March of their juvenile career, are said to be 'forward'.

FOUNDING SIRES The Darley Arabian, Byerly Turk and Godolphin Barb. Every thoroughbred can be traced back to one of these three founding sires.

FREE When a horse uses up too much energy by pulling hard at the start of a race, he is said to be 'free'. This is generally a negative trait in a horse and usually means that they compromise their chance of winning or being placed.

FRONT-RUNNER A horse that prefers to race in front.

FURLONG A distance of 220 yards. There are eight furlongs in one mile. Races around the world are run in metres. One mile is 1600m.

G

GALLOP REPORTS These are featured in the Racing Post, the Weekender and Raceform publications. Each paper will have a correspondent watching horses on the gallops in the major training centres such as Newmarket, Lambourn, Middleham and Malton.

GELDING A male horse that has been castrated.

GENUINE A horse that always seems to try hard to win a race is said to be 'genuine'.

GOING State of the ground; firm, good to firm, good, good to soft, soft and heavy. All-Weather tracks are generally described as 'standard', but are occasionally deemed 'slow' or 'fast'.

GONE IN THE COAT A horse's wellbeing can often be decided by the state of their skin. If the coat is shiny and bright, the chances are the horse is fit and well. If the coat is dull, grey and dusty-looking, then the horse may perform below par.

GOOD DOER A horse that eats well and without fuss.

GOOD WALKER If a horse is a fine walker, e.g. he has a long, precise stride, the chances are he will be an attractive galloper. A horse should overstep the footprint made with his foreleg with his hind leg on every step to be a good walker. This is known as 'tracking up.'

GRADED RACES The jumping equivalent of Group races on the Flat, providing top-class, competitive racing. There are grades of 1 to 3 for the very best horses.

GRAND £1,000.

GREEN A horse that shows inexperience when racing.

GROOMS Stable employees that are responsible for riding and caring for the horses on a daily basis.

GROUP RACES Highly-competitive Flat races over a variety of distances, divided into three groups (1,2,3).

GUINEA British gold coin taken out of circulation in 1813, worth 21 shillings (£1.05p in today's money).

HALF BROTHER/SISTER Two horses are half brothers/sisters if they are out of the same dam, but are by different stallions. Two horses by the same stallion but different dams are NOT deemed half relations, as there are so many of them.

HAND The unit of measurement for horses. A hand is four inches.

HANDICAP A handicap race aims to create a level playing field amongst the runners. This is achieved by giving the horses an official handicap rating. In a handicap race, those horses with a higher rating carry more weight, those with a lower rating carry less weight.

HANDICAPPER 1) A horse that tends to race solely in handicaps rather than other types of races or 2) a person appointed by the British Horseracing Authority (BHA) to allocate a rating for a horse. That rating then converts to the weight the horse must carry in a handicap race.

HANGING Horses will often veer, or 'hang' either left or right when they become tired at the end of a race, or don't like the ground, for instance.

HEAD LAD The person in charge of running a training yard on a day-to-day basis.

HEADQUARTERS Newmarket. The place of the former Jockey Club Headquarters.

HEDGING Placing a second bet to reduce the liability of the first bet.

HERITAGE HANDICAP The leading handicaps of the Flat season, which tend to be well-established, valuable handicap races with prize money in excess of £50,000.

HOMEBRED A horse bred by its owner.

HORSERACE BETTING LEVY BOARD This board was founded in 1961 after the legalisation of off-course betting. The Levy Board provides the sport with a major source of finance, which it collects from every bookmaker.

HUNTER CHASE A race for horses that are qualified to race in point-to-points in the UK or Ireland. They are for amateur riders and are usually open to licensed trainers. The biggest races in the calendar are the Foxhunter's run at both Cheltenham and Aintree.

IBAS Independent Betting Arbitration Service. They settle disputes between bookmakers and punters, assuming that the bookmaker is a member of IBAS. (Their address is P.O. Box 4011, London, E14 5BB).

IN THE FRAME If a horse is 'in the frame,' it means he has been placed in a race.

J

JOCKED OFF A jockey loses a ride to another jockey.

JOCKEY CLUB The Jockey Club is dedicated to improving the sport and investing in its future. Profits generated by The Jockey Club's businesses, such as its fourteen racecourses, training grounds and the National Stud are re-invested back into racing.

JOLLY The favourite.

L

LAY To lay a horse is to take money (a bet) for it on the basis that you think it will not win. This is the opposite of backing a horse to win.

LAY UP (in running) When a horse is keeping in touch with the leaders during a race, it is said to be 'laying up'.

LAYERS The bookmakers.

LENGTH One length is the equivalent of the distance from a horse's nose to its tail, and is the distance used to separate finishers in a result of a race. Other smaller distances are a nose, a short head, a head, a neck, half a length and three-quarters of a length.

LEVEL STAKES A punter's staking procedure, where he places an identical unit (amount of stake/money) on each of his selections.

LISTED RACE These are races which fall just below Group 3 level. They are an opportunity for horses that are better than handicappers, but not quite Group class, to gain some 'black type'.

LONG HANDICAP Horses that are rated below the minimum weight for a particular race are therefore inconvenienced by carrying more weight due to their low handicap mark. They are said to be 'out of the handicap'.

LOT A group of horses ridden out on the gallops together at a trainer's yard.

M

MAIDEN RACES For horses who have not won that particular category of race e.g. a maiden on the Flat may have won over hurdles. Likewise, a horse that has won on the Flat can run in maiden hurdles or chases.

MARE A female horse aged five years or over.

MATCH A two-horse race. A famous example would be the Newmarket Challenge Whip, which is held annually between two horses owned by Members of The Jockey Club, without prize money.

MEDIAN AUCTION RACE Races on the Flat that are restricted to the progeny of stallions whose offspring's sale price does not exceed the figure specified in the race conditions, when passing through public auction.

MICROCHIPPING Every foal born has a microchip inserted underneath its skin, which shows an identification number when scanned. This ensures that the wrong horse is never allowed to race.

MINOR HONOURS Horses that achieve the 'minor honours' are those that have been placed second, third and occasionally fourth in certain races.

MONKEY betting parlance for the amount of £500.

NATIONAL HUNT Or 'Jump racing', is racing over obstacles. Horses may race over hurdles, fences or in 'bumpers'. Hurdles are three and a half foot tall obstacles that can be knocked flat if hit hard. These obstacles tend to suit horses coming from Flat racing, as there is plenty of emphasis on speed and not so much on jumping technique. Racing over steeplechase fences is more complicated. Horses must have much more respect for the larger obstacles, which vary in height, width and stiffness from course to course.

NOMINATION This is a breeding right; a nomination to a particular stallion is purchased by the mare's owner some way in advance, then the mare is sent to stud to meet that stallion in order to become pregnant. The stud fee is then normally paid to the stud should the broodmare be scanned in foal by 1st October.

NON TRIER Horses that are believed to have been stopped or held back in their races to prevent them from obtaining the best possible position. The BHA offer very heavy penalties if anyone is found guilty of 'not trying to obtain the best possible placing'.

NOT OFF A horse that is thought not to have been allowed to run on its merits.

NOVICE (1) A two-year-old Flat horse that has not won more than two races. (2) A novice horse, e.g. a novice hurdler, is deemed a novice if they have not won a race over hurdles before the start of the current season (the season tends to run until the last weekend in April, and restarts the following Monday). If the horse has won on or after March 1st of the previous season, he may continue to race as a novice until 31 October of the next season. The horse will remain a novice over fences if he has only won over hurdles, and vice versa, regardless of how successful he is. Horses are likely to incur a penalty in these races for each win, although the size of the penalty differs from race to race, according to the class of the previous race won and the race the horse is entered in.

NURSERIES Handicaps for two-year-olds.

OBLIGE A horse that wins a race has 'obliged.'

ODDS Devised centuries ago before decimalisation. For example, the return on a 11/10 winner would be £1 and one florin, a 5/4 winner would yield a £1 and 2 half crowns, etc. An 11/10 winner today would return £1.10 to a £1 stake.

ODDS AGAINST A bookmaker returns a dividend worth more than your stake on a winning bet, plus your stake.

ODDS ON A bookmaker returns a dividend worth less than your stake on a winning bet. He also returns your stake.

ON THE BRIDLE A horse going well during a race. There is no need for the jockey to persuade the horse to go faster, as he is happy with his position.

ON THE NOD Horses heads move up and down as they gallop. In close finishes, a photograph is taken to decide the winner. Some finishes are so tight, the winner is simply the horse that has his neck stretched out at the right time.

OVER ROUND The bookmaker's margin in excess of 100% on a race, ensuring that if a punter backed each horse, he would be unable to be in profit.

OVER THE TOP A horse who has had a long, hard season of racing or training, and is no longer in peak form.

OVER WEIGHT Excess of the weight carried when the jockey is too heavy to ride at the weight designated in the race conditions.

PASSPORT Weatherbys give each horse a personal document when they are registered and microchipped as foals. The passport must remain with the horse for life, and must accompany him whenever he travels to the racecourse. This ensures that two horses can never be confused. The racecourse vet carries a microchip scanner, which gives a reading that must match the passport.

PATTERN Listed races, Group races and Graded races over obstacles.

PENALTY Extra weight carried for a recent previous win.

PERMIT HOLDER Trainers who only handle their own horses or those owned by their immediate family. They are only able to run horses under National Hunt rules.

PIN HOOKING The buying of foals with the intention of selling them as yearlings to make a profit.

PITCH A precise place allocated in the Betting Ring at a racecourse for each bookmaker to set up his stand. Pitches used to be allocated by seniority, but are now sold to the highest bidder.

PLATE Most racehorses run in aluminium 'plates' rather than the more traditional steel shoes as they are lighter.

PLATER A horse that tends to run in Selling or Claiming races.

POINT A whole unit of odds. A horse that has been backed from 6/1 into 5/1 for example, is said to have 'come in a point'.

POINT-TO-POINT They are steeplechases for horses ridden by amateur riders and trained by unlicensed trainers. Races start at the end of November and run until early June. They are organised by local hunts or clubs and take place all over the UK and Ireland.

PONY £25

PRESS ASSOCIATION Is responsible for notifying bookmakers, newspapers and other media of any news within the sport industry, including results. Their announced result is the one that bookmakers will pay out on, whether or not it is universally agreed. For instance, if there was a dispute about which football player scored in a football match, their decision would be the one that decides payouts.

PUNDIT A horse racing critic or commentator. They are also known as 'hacks'.

PUSHED OUT A horse that has only had to be 'pushed out' is one that wins fairly easily, without the use of the whip.

QUARTERS The large muscled area around a horse's pelvis that is largely responsible for propelling the horse forward.

R

RACE SECTIONAL The most efficient way for a horse to win a race (assuming the course is flat) is to maintain the same speed throughout (and finish in front). Sectional times show at which point in a race the runners went slower and faster. For instance, if the horses ran very fast in the first two furlongs but slowed down towards the finish, the times can quantify this assumption. Using race times can add merit to a horse's performance, and is the foundation of some tipster's betting sdvice.

RAG An outsider in the betting market.

RAILS BOOKMAKER The only bookmakers permitted in the Members' Enclosure at a racecourse. They are situated on the rails between the Members and Tattersalls enclosures. It is only recently that rails bookmakers have been permitted to display their prices. Previously, they had to shout their prices to attract attention.

RAN OUT A horse that leaves the designated route of the race, thereby terminating his participation.

RANGY A horse with a long frame that he will fill as he matures.

RATED STAKES Valuable handicaps with a rating and weight range limit. For instance, the top weight may only carry a stone more than the bottom weight in most rated stakes races.

REFUSE A horse that refused to jump an obstacle despite their rider intending to jump it. The horse is not eliminated from the race unless the jockey falls off, in which case he is forbidden to remount.

RETAINER Many owners and trainers pay a particular jockey to ride as a priority for them.

RING INSPECTOR When a dispute arises between a bookmaker and a punter at a racecourse, the Ring Inspector helps resolve the situation.

RINGER These scams should no longer occur thanks to the introduction of passports and microchips, but previously, an unscrupulous person would declare a horse to run in a race and then send a different horse (who is usually either much better or more experienced than the one declared) and then back it heavily, hoping the horse will win and the scam will be pulled off.

RULE 4 When a horse is withdrawn without coming under starters' orders and a new betting market cannot be formed, a Rule 4 deduction will apply to all bets if the withdrawn horse went to post at less than 14/1.

RUNNER A person employed by a bookmaker who will record bets, check other bookmakers' prices and alter them as and when necessary in a betting market. They may also be required to place bets with other bookmakers. With computerised betting and computerised bookmakers' boards, runners can do their jobs much quicker and easier now.

S

SADDLE CLOTH Or number cloth; this displays the racecard number of the horse and must be worn by all runners.

SCHOOLING The training of a horse to jump safely and efficiently.

SCOPE A horse has 'scope' if he looks likely to mature further and improve during his career.

SCOPE Endoscopic examination of horse, to check for blood or mucus in the lungs to help ensure the horse is at peak condition. Possibly also to check whether there is an obstruction that requires an operation to improve a horse's breathing.

SCORE £20

SCRATCHED A horse whose entry for a race has been cancelled.

SCRUBBED ALONG The jockey pushing vigorously with his hands and kicking with his legs to urge the horse on.

SELLING RACES These are the lowest grade of race. After a selling race, the winner is offered for sale by auction in the Winners' Enclosure. Any other runner in the race can be claimed for a fee set at the entry stage of the race.

SIRE Father of a horse.

S I S Satellite Information Services.

SNATCHED UP A horse that is hampered during a race, e.g. another horse crosses his path, forcing the jockey to alter his path. This reduces momentum and inhibits the horse's winning chance.

SORE SHINS Younger horses can get sore shins in their training or after racing on firm ground. Sore shins can be a way that a horse tells its trainer it's being trained too hard.

S.P. Starting Price. The odds that all SP bets are settled at.

SPREADING A PLATE A horse losing a shoe.

SPRING DOUBLE The Grand National and the Lincoln.

SPRINTER Horses that are specialists in five and six-furlong races.

SPRINGER A horse whose betting odds are reducing rapidly.

STALLION An entire male horse kept at stud for breeding purposes.

STAYER Horses that are more effective over longer distances, e.g. one mile and six furlongs and over on the Flat, and three miles plus over Jumps.

STEAMER A horse that has been backed furiously on the morning of a race.

STEWARDS Employed by the BHA to ensure that their rules are enforced. Raceday stewards ensure that no wrongdoing occurs during the day's races, and will hold an enquiry should they be unhappy with the performance of any jockey, trainer or owner. Raceday stewards differ from course to course, and usually tend to make a disciplinary action on the day, or refer the offender to the BHA headquarters. Jockeys may be banned for minor whip or interference cases, or sent to HQ for more serious cases of non-triers, etc. The result of each race is always decided on the day, and is the result bookmakers pay out on.

STEWARDS' ENQUIRY Signified by a bell ringing straight after each race, which warns bookmakers not to pay out. Bets should be settled after 'Weighed In' is announced, which means placings have remained unaltered.

STORE HORSE A young horse that has not yet been trained, to allow it time to mature.

STRIKE RATE The ratio of winners to losers. Trainers' and jockeys' strike rates are published regularly in The Racing Post.

SUPPLEMENTED For big races, horses can be entered early on and at several 'forfeit stages' they have the option to discontinue their entry by forfeiting the entry fees paid by that stage. Where other horses wish to be entered close to the big race and have therefore not been paying the previous stages of entry fees, these late entrants must pay a larger sum (the supplement) in order to be entered into the race. This is very costly (£75,000 for the Epsom Derby) with no guarantee of success!

SWEEPSTAKES A race where entry fees, forfeits, etc, go to the winner and the placed horses.

TAILED OFF A horse that is so far behind the leaders in a race that it is totally out of contention.

THINKER A horse that has his own ideas about racing is regarded as a 'thinker.'

TISSUES The prices at which the betting market is forecast to open at, which are prepared by a betting and form expert.

TON £100

TONGUE TIE An elasticated tie that holds the horse's tongue flat in the mouth, therefore keeping the passage for air intake open and stopping the horse from 'swallowing' its tongue. Tongue ties must be declared at the declaration stage.

TRAINED ON A horse that has held its form from season to season. For example, some two-year-olds who have been busy as juveniles will show no worthwhile form after the winter break, but those who continue to show form are said to have 'trained on'.

TRAVELLING A horse that is 'on the bridle' i.e. is running comfortably and either holding a position or making up ground with little or no effort required from the jockey.

TRIP The distance of a race.

TURN OF FOOT A burst of speed that a horse can apply when needed to win a race.

TWO-YEAR-OLD The minimum age for a horse to begin its racing career is two years. All racehorses have a 'birthday' on 1st January each year so it is possible that a 'two-year-old' is not actually 24 months from the date it was born. Some leading trainers have a policy never to run a juvenile until they are genuinely two-years-old.

UNFURNISHED Weak and immature-looking horses who have yet to fill their frames. They may be long, leggy individuals that need to put on more muscle and condition.

UPSIDES Horses are ridden alongside each other, generally nose to nose in training or racing. When young horses first start to be trained, going 'upsides' is often very daunting for them but they need to get used to running close to other horses.

VALET A person employed to look after a jockey's clothing and equipment at the races and to assist him throughout the day.

VIRUS A contagious condition likely to affect a horse's health and running performance. They are often difficult to detect until a horse has raced as some viruses don't show up in pre-race tests.

WALK OVER A one-horse race. The horse is only required to breeze past the stands and is not required to race.

WARN OFF A person that fails to pay fees in the horseracing industry, or has been guilty of severe wrong-doing will be 'warned off' by the BHA. They will be unable to attend any race meeting or set foot on Jockey Club property until their period of exclusion has lapsed.

WEAVER A horse that moves his head from side to side repeatedly when in his stable. This is a nervous trait, just like crib-biting and box-walking.

WEIGHED IN Once signalled at a racecourse, the result of the race on the day cannot be changed. This will not be announced until the time for objections has lapsed, stewards' enquiries have been considered and jockeys have weighed back in to ensure they have ridden at the correct weight.

WEIGHED OUT A practice that every jockey must undertake before being allowed to race. The jockey must present himself and all of his equipment, excluding his helmet and whip, to the Clerk of the Scales, who will check that he is the correct weight as published in the racecard. If the jockey cannot ride at the correct weight, he is able to put up 'overweight', which is naturally a hindrance to the horse's chances.

WEIGHT CLOTH This is a leather cloth that contains pockets for extra weight (usually lead) to be added if the jockey is not heavy enough to make the weight the horse must carry.

WEIGHT FOR AGE A scale is published by the BHA, and determines how much weight the younger horses will receive from older horses at a particular time of year in WFA races, such as the Eclipse or the Arc, for instance.

WIND OPERATION A process where a horse's breathing is improved using corrective surgery. These are very common in NH horses and can improve performance remarkably.

WORK Training a horse on the gallops.

WORKMANLIKE A capable horse that looks well suited to racing and can continue winning or running well, albeit possibly with his jockey working hard to do so.

YEARLING A one-year-old horse. Foals become yearlings after 1st January regardless of which month they were born in.